Fairy Tales with a Mexican Twist

Fairy Tales with a Mexican Twist

SOUL STORIES

Jacqueline Gerson

Illustrations by Saúl Kaminer

fisher king press

Fairy Tales with a Mexican Twist
Soul Stories
Copyright © 2019 by Jacqueline Gerson
First Edition
ISBN 978-1-77169-046-1 Paperback
ISBN 978-1-77169-047-8 eBook

Published in the United States of America by Fisher King Press, an imprint of Fisher King Enterprises. For information on obtaining permission for use of material from this work, submit a written request to:

permissions@fisherkingpress.com

Fisher King Press
www.fisherkingpress.com
+1-307-222-9575

Many thanks to all who have directly or indirectly provided permission to quote their works. Every effort has been made to trace all copyright holders; however, if any have been overlooked, the respective authors will be pleased to make the necessary arrangements at the first opportunity.

CONTENTS

With much love, this book is dedicated to:

Valeria

Gabriela

Jeremy

Emily

Their joy in play
and the magic they find in every day life
are a gift, a divine inspiration.

Acknowledgements

I would like to start by expressing my gratitude to all the people who over the years, have shared with me their most intimate truths, hidden pains, and scary corners of their soul. Through their process, they have also revealed new and highly creative possibilities of living life. Their openness and trust are an inspiration for the courage needed to live. To all of them, whose names are kept in the most sacred confidentiality, my deepest gratitude.

I would like to mention Dr. Thomas Kirsch for his constant presence and belief in me. The editorial advice of Dr. John Beebe, as well as his vision for seeing in me, years ago, the Jungian analyst I became. Dr. Susan Thackery's poetic ability for naming soul's matters has been most helpful in the development of this book. Dr. Joan Chodorow with whom transcendental matters were discovered. Jesus Manrique who makes the cold language of computers seem friendly. Rocío Vega for her help with endless paper work. Dr. Francisco Gonzalez de Cossio for his encouragement and guidance. Finally, the authors of many wonderful books who dared writing their inner most truth—they are an inspiration.

My lifelong friend and colleague, Claude Juvin has believed in my work in the blurriest of times. Her trust and capacity in finding meaning in the descent and recognizing and celebrating the return has been a significant support.

Working with Saúl Kaminer has been a pleasure. His deep sensitivity and resonance in translating the stories into his beautiful pictoric language became a re-discovery of the very same stories. For sharing his art, energy and friendship, my deepest gratitude.

To my dearest Ricardo and Erika, I feel most proud and deeply joyful for them being in my life. Their ever-present love is a most meaningful source of courage and strength.

Dr. Salomon Fainsilber with whom I create a story every day. He walks by my side and holds my hand in the adventure of life.

To the sunsets and the infallible first rays at dawn. To the moon's mystery and the magic in stars. To the movement and sound of the ocean. To nature's nurturing and healing power. To the endless beauty of flowers. To the strength of the wind and its aliveness. To my ever passion in dance. To music's soul language. To the new and enlivening vision art brings. To dream's wisdom and the spark of imagination. To the sweet and sour, the light and dark and for the privilege of being alive, I am deeply grateful.

Comments on the Drawings and their Relation to the Text

It was a privilege making the drawings for the 13 stories of the book *Fairy Tales with a Mexican Twist* written by Jacqueline Gerson.

It has been a creative challenge to interpret the stories and to give shape through colors, forms, and lines. By interpret, I mean it has not only been an illustration but a real work of active imagination that emerged from the stories.

The way I read the stories was very peculiar. I got to know them through working sessions in which Jacqueline Gerson read them in Spanish while she was translating from English. At the same time, I was drawing images inspired by the readings.

I must say that the emotion that was transmitted through the reading of the stories was strong. I felt that for her, it was as if she was reliving the ideas and feelings that led her the need to write them. In an automatic and simultaneous way, I tried to draw the emotion that was being expressed. Such is the tradition of surrealistic automatism, which consists of drawing while connected to the emotion rather than through a mental process.

This work could be the beginning of a resilience or healing process, where the written and the visual interact. Participating in this project has been a very enriching and creative experience, which has nurtured my own creative process. For this, I am deeply grateful to Jacqueline Gerson.

Saúl Kaminer
October 2018

Story telling reveals meaning without committing the error of defining it.

—Hannah Arendt

BAND-AIDS

This story takes place in the far-off and isolated Land of Believe. It is the story of a special wise old man who was able to heal the strangest symptoms arising from totally unknown diseases that no one else could cure. People from all over the world who could afford to travel to the Land of Believe would do so looking for a cure to what other healers, not knowing what to do, had refused to treat. The old man was especially known for his ability to help children, those little ones who, for some peculiar and unknown reason, were unable to live a healthy, happy life.

He lived in a small house in the woods. It was surrounded by huge trees, which hid it from view. One had to really want to get there in order to find the place. The front door of the house opened to a little vestibule. It was here that any adults accompanying a child would be asked to wait while the child was taken into the house by a plump, kindly, elderly matron, who welcomed the children warmly as she ushered them into a bright, spacious room, flooded with sunlight which streamed in through an enormous skylight.

Many children had come through this special room. Among them was a girl whose eyelashes wouldn't stop growing. More often than not, the child was unable to see through such long lashes. Cutting them didn't help, and, indeed, doing this only made them grow even faster and thicker than ever, until they finally covered her beautiful pale blue eyes entirely, preventing her from seeing the world around her.

Another child that arrived was a boy whose only delight was to dig holes in the earth and then crawl into them and remain there. Not only was he unable to come out of his own accord, but he would crouch there alone and cry until someone, usually an angry adult, came to drag him out. He would repeat this unusual game every single day, no matter how frightened he had been previously as a result of the experience.

Oh! And there was the cutest five-year-old girl who was brought in because she was unable to walk. The skin on the soles of her feet had become thinner and thinner as she kept walking. And the thinner it got, the more sensitive and sore her feet became, up to the point where she was literally unable to stand, let alone walk.

I must also mention the girl who had flowers growing out of her ears. When this happened for the first time, the adults thought that the girl was sticking the flowers into her ears herself. But before long, they realized that this was not so. It became abundantly clear that the flowers were actually growing out of her ears, and the more the flowers grew, the less she was able to hear.

These children, and many more over the years, came to be healed in the room, under the enormous skylight through which the intense blue sky could be seen quite clearly. No one knew in advance how long each child would remain in the room, but even more intriguing was the question of what they were doing inside while they were there. Were they playing? If so, with what? After the children came out, they would be questioned by the adults about what they had been doing while they were inside the room, and all of them, no matter what their particular ailment, would invariably have the same answer: "I was playing with Band-Aids."

"With Band-Aids?" the mystified adults would respond to this simple but honest reply. "What Band-Aids? What do you mean 'Band-Aids'? The usual Band-Aids?"

"Well, there were all kinds of Band-Aids in all shapes and sizes, and they had all the colors of the rainbow. It was so much fun! But also, if you wanted one that they didn't have, you could make it yourself. And that was even more fun! You could use all kinds of materials to create new Band-Aids. It was so much fun that we all wanted to try making our own, and then of course we would wear them ourselves, or share them with our newly made friends! We got to see all the new designs that the other children had made, and it was fun to try them on for a while, but most of us would end up wearing our own, because they felt much more comfortable for us!"

The adults were amazed at the simplicity of what the children were reporting. They would wonder, is it true that we came all this way to the Land of Believe just for the children to play—and not just play, but play with nothing more than Band-Aids? The matron would bring out milk and cookies for the children, and tea for the adults. When it was time to leave, they would be even more astonished to see the old man appear and say to them, "Hello, so nice to meet you. Thank you for bringing your children, I always learn so much from them. Children teach me how to go on playing, and the wonderful art of healing, so I just want to say how grateful I am to you for bringing your children to the Land of Believe, and I hope you have a safe journey back home. Goodbye, and enjoy your marvelous children." Having said these words, he would leave through a small door and go into his quarters, while the matron helped the children with their coats and mittens and hugged them goodbye.

On the way back home, the adults would wonder if the healing method described by the children would have any effect on the strange symptoms that had initially brought them to the Land of Believe. They would each go back home hoping that a miracle would occur and their children would eventually be cured, as so many others had been before them.

A long time passed. No one was able to tell how long, but there was an important change in the children who had been taken to the Land of Believe. Let me tell you what happened with these children.

The girl with the beautiful blue eyes and very long eyelashes became a painter. Oh, yes! No one was able to perceive light and shadow the way she did. Peering through her long eyelashes, she was able to capture a spectrum of colors that had never been seen before. When asked how she was able to create such interesting hues with such depth and sensitivity, she would simply answer: "It is my eyelashes that allow me to see the world in such a special way. It is in between eyelashes that I discover what is unseen by others. At times, my eyelashes seem to be in the way. There seems to be a lot of black in the world, and I have to make a great effort to see anything at all. But it is precisely then that I also discover the depth in the world and in my work. I discover the luminosity that arises in the darkness of my vision. Actually, my eyelashes allow me to play with the light and the shadow. It is intense work, so I have a ritual for closing a working session whenever I get tired before returning home. I have some milk and cookies just before I put on my coat and mittens. That soothes my soul after a long, hard day."

Then there was the boy who used to dig holes in the earth and crawl into them. Well, he went on digging, but now he looked for gold and silver, for he had become a miner! He did not do it alone. He had a team

with whom he dug huge holes and then went down into them looking for precious metals. But before going down into the big organized hole, he had a special ritual that he repeated every time. He would look into the blue sky and say to himself: "I know that this intense blue sky will be waiting here for me, in the same place and the same way, to receive me once again on the surface of the earth when I come back, and no matter how deep I go, I will always take the blue sky with me, for it lives in my mind and in my soul. I will be out with the help of my friends as we join each other in our task, and as soon as I return to the surface of the earth, the first thing I will see will be the blue sky, which will be there waiting for me each time." With his ritual performed, he was able to do his work in a trusting and rewarding manner, and his trust grew each day as he found the blue sky waiting for him when he emerged from within the earth.

As for the girl whose soles became thinner and thinner as she walked, making walking extremely painful, well, she became a ballerina. That was truly a miracle. One day, as she was playing, pretending to be a princess dancing with her imaginary prince, she discovered that she could stand on her toes. This gave the soles of her feet a chance to get off the ground, and be surrounded by lots of air, which helped them breathe. When she would finally get back down on the soles of her feet, they wouldn't hurt so much anymore since they had had a chance to rest from contact with the at-times-too-dense earth. And of course, she would get blisters on her toes like any other ballerina would, but she always carried her Band-Aids with her, and she was a master at using them to heal her blisters as well as to protect her toes when they began to feel too tired from the weight they had to bear. She learned to combine walking with dancing. In fact, she was able to practically dance as she walked in order to move through life in a careful, graceful manner.

The other little girl, the one who had to deal with the burden of flowers growing out of her ears—she learned to differentiate between the harsh, intrusive voices that would deafen her, by blocking her ears with "flowery" but insincere words and the almost inaudible voices that were begging to be heard but were drowned out in the midst of louder imposing sounds. She became a childcare worker—a childcare worker who could hear the most seemingly inconsequential but nevertheless deeply important things that children had to say. She loved to play with them as she took care of every child, and from time to time, a flower would pop out of her ear, and she, together with the children would all laugh with delight at the comical sight, which was her very unique contribution to humor and laughter. There was no other childcare worker who could make them feel so happy in such a simple and spontaneous way. Opening her ears to listen to them and her heart to love them, she was able to laugh at herself and share the joy of discovering what she liked doing the most—playing with children. It was only in this environment that the flowers growing out of her ears did not block her hearing, but instead enhanced the joy of creative play.

All these children, who eventually became brave adults daring to live life to the fullest, would, from time to time, return to the Land of Believe, where they would once again play with Band-Aids. As they did when they were children, they would create new Band-Aids because life had taught them that as we go on living, new wounds crop up, and we need, from time to time, to update our old Band-Aids to fit our new needs. So they would experiment with colors and shapes, materials and textures, and imagine all sorts of possibilities until they came up with one that suited that particular moment in their life, one that felt comfortable, one that made them feel at home, no matter where they were. Then, they would put on their coats and mittens and return home with the newly acquired knowledge that allowed them to get on with their lives in a meaningful and joyous way.

COLOR WRONG

Once upon a time, there was a rich and interesting kingdom named Color Land. In this special place, honoring its name, there were all kinds of colors, many of them known by most anybody, and some were distinct tones rarely seen anywhere else. In the kingdom, there was an old legend that had been told for many, many years to uncountable generations. The legend was about how Color Land came into being and how special the kingdom was, since no matter how many colors existed in this particular land, there were always new tones appearing. This could only happen, however, as long as people continued to believe in the richness ingrained in color—then possibilities were endless.

The inhabitants of Color Land, each and every one of them, had a name not only by which to be known, but more important, that exact name reflected how their view of the world was tinted. For each of them, it was that same abundant and deep color that would appear in every situation in Color Land in which they participated. Among the population, accordingly, there were inhabitants named Color Soft, Color Fair, Color Intense, Color Sour, Color Pleasure, Color Shiny, Color Humble, Color Dreamy, and as many more as there were inhabitants to fulfill their names. One of the inhabitants was a naive and tender young man who was known for having a most peculiar and deeply ingrained color tone, which had been inherited and held impeccable for many generations. His name was Color Wrong.

Color Wrong saw what his own assigned name dictated him to see in all the situations in which he participated. He truly believed that the whole kingdom, and every single inhabitant he knew within it, as well as every happening he had managed to witness in Color Land, had the wrong color ingrained.

One morning, when all Colors were resting from work and school, some of them went outside to play and chatting their endless discussion of how life was tinted differently for each of them. Such talk had been going on forever in Color Land, as each inhabit kept defending his or her very own color tone. As her name suggested, Color Pleasure spoke about all the types of pleasures she had known in life. She was able to see pleasure not only in a clear blue sky, but also in a stormy, gray, endless rainy day. She often spoke about the pleasure that she took in nature's strength, to which Color Soft would reply saying that the generalization held only while nature stays soft, tender, and slow, since for Color Soft, that was the only condition under which she could get to touch the essence of anything alive. Color Intense would disagree because he had the opposite understanding of life and what it allowed us to experience in innermost nature, but before he could finish making that point, Color Fair intervened saying that though it is fair to give one's point of view, because one has a right to be faithful to one self, it is fair to change one's mind, and also fair to disagree, which of course left Color Intense nowhere. Color Intense reacted answering back that neither nature nor life can be halfways—it is always one way or the other. Life, he concluded, is intense and anything real that happens in life will be equally intense. Color Humble wisely said, each of us don't have the ultimate truth. No one can affirm that what any of us sees is absolutely right because there is more than one way to see, to know, and to understand. What all of us see is more than what any single color may grasp, to which Color Sour added, and therefore, we will never get to know the truth, if it exists at all.

So, he counseled, don't even try seeing more than you already can, we are Colors and Colors only, and our fate is to remain as such and never to become anything more than our particular tint on things. Speaking last in this argument was Color Dreamy, who, as always was a bit in her dreams. She said, one doesn't really know what will be, but everybody needs to have a dream, and everybody needs to fight for their particular dream, because believing in one's dreams is the way to life itself.

Color Wrong did not participate in this conversation because he hadn't gone outside. Getting some sun and breathing some fresh air were both very wrong—anyone could see that. He thought that talking, playing, and resting without doing anything that might be considered important, was certainly wrong. He would rather stay home and work, even though, according to his perception, his own work would never end up being good enough for him. Like everything else, it was wrong, and his efforts to do it as well as possible, could never be sufficient since he knew from experience that things that were done, whether by him or anyone else, so far from turning out acceptably, always ended up being wrong.

On that particular day, when the colors that had gone outside were discussing their different perspectives on life, a very intense light crossed through the sky. The light was shiny, brilliant and beautiful, and had lots of sparkles coming out of it. The inhabitants of Color Land were enchantedly observing this light, the likes of which they had never seen before. So impressed they were, that they just couldn't take their eyes away from the sky. Time stood still. Being caught in such an amazing vision, their eyes became filled with the sparkles coming from the light, and as they took them in, they found that they were hardly able to go on seeing anything else in the usual way. It had become absolutely impossible for any of them to distinguish anything that resembled color once their eyes were filled with sparkles. It soon became obvious that after this strange visitation, the people in Color Land had become color blind.

When the inhabitants of Color Land were able to resume the discussion which they were having before this phenomenon had taken place, they were unaware that the color with which they had seen the world, until then, had been lost. Being accustomed to the endless and constant speeches given by each of the colors defending his or her particular view of the world, it was Color Wrong who noticed that things had changed. Although not blinded the way the other colors were, even Color Wrong hardly recognized them. He had always felt that Color Land and its inhabitants were wrong-headed, but this time, their world seemed to be at its worst. Without colors, even if they were the wrong colors, chaos prevailed and Color Wrong found himself to be the sole right seeing witness of the confused, dark and messy situation that had become Color Land.

Not realizing that they had become color blind, the rest of the inhabitants began to come playfully closer to each other, not only in their discussions about their different views of the world, but for the first time known for that generation, in daring to be in physical contact with each other. This was something they had previously been extremely careful not to let happen because they knew very well, that coming to be in contact with each other might contaminate the purity of one's very own tone. Now that they were blind to color, they could experiment with being closer to each other. Feeling that it was safe, they even dared mixing and matching their colors, which until then had had to remain separate in order to stay permanent. It was no longer necessary, since it had become impossible to see, for a color to remain as absolute as possible. The colors no longer had to be proudly carried all alone in their lives, and thus the world they had seen before began to change around them. Although they did not know it, the inhabitants of Color Land were engaged in actualizing the legend that existed for generations—the many possibilities of viewing life, and that new tones held within themselves would one day emerge in various tints, allowing a complexity of colors to permeate each Color Land inhabitant's vision of the world.

While Color Wrong was quick to point out the obfuscation that accompanied the prevailing chaos, the other Colors, though admittedly in the midst of confusion, were beginning to feel a tiny new light, this time, not in the sky, but arising from within themselves. As Color Wrong could clearly see, the Colors went on carefully touching each other thus blending their tints, and they even seemed to be joyful about this confusing endeavor. Knowing it would be wrong to share such a thought with the Colors that were clearly enjoying themselves, Color Wrong said to himself, "How wrong is all this! They must have lost their minds! Of course I will remain pure, because I know touching and mixing among Colors is very wrong. I will keep being faithful to my own color. Even the world has never been as wrong as I see it today, oh, it is wrong, very wrong—completely wrong!! And I can stay true to my vision of that." Color Wrong went on proudly repeating his current view of Color Land, which had the appeal to him of being consistent with the values he had always been able to hold.

Time passed and the rest of the Colors in Color Land began recovering their individual visions, until finally, once again, each of them was able to identify colors. But they could also see that things had indeed changed. Even though they tried very hard to focus as before, they couldn't see the way they were used to seeing. The greatest revelation from such a profound experience which each of them could verify, was not understanding what had happened, not seeing the same as they were used to seeing, and had made them look not only at the world outside, but at themselves. So, though the world was indeed not seen as before, even more significant was the fact that for the first time they had learned how to turn their views inside toward themselves. When they did so, the inhabitants of Color Land made an incredible discovery—they found that, not only was the color through which they saw the world different, it was now clear that color was coming from within themselves. With this realization, the Colors slowly got to discover that beyond color, they had actually found a new dimension of experience. They had discovered depth.

Before depth perception entered their ken, it had only been the world's nature that for years was debated. The question of "who" was actually looking at the world that was colored in the way it was perceived had essentially been omitted. Facing this question now, feelings of surprise, shame, remorse, and discomfort arose among the inhabitants of Color Land. They kept trying to reverse what they had done. With the discovery of depth, feelings of embarrassment, uncertainty, and disorientation arouse in relation to the vision they had had of the world. Little did they notice the tiny new light that was now shining within them; its function was not to leave them color blind, but to help them see through their former blindness and even their shame about that. The steady little light slowly led them to feel more confident in what now appeared so very strange.

But even now, there was also Color Wrong, claiming to see a world that went on being wrong, nurtured in fact by the fresh wrongness he saw in his fellow inhabitants who had all lost their original natural colors and their characteristic views of the world. For him, to discover the other Colors was not only wrong but the possibility of discovering oneself through another was absolutely uncomprehending. Little could he see that his world had in fact changed, and though he was right in his perception, he was still fatally lacking depth. Worst of all, he had no small inner guiding light to allow him to see that the otherness around him could also be right.

Life for the inhabitants of Color Land had thus become different for everybody. Although most of the Colors went on looking and discovering themselves through the discovery of the other, Color Wrong went on finding only more wrongness in the new tones that kept appearing around him as never before seen. He hadn't changed his view of the world and proudly carried his name to its fulfillment, even though at times, he got to be called Color Blind. He knew that was not true. He had never been blind, not even for a bit of time, like the rest. He had no reason to doubt that his was the only enduring truth. Because of this, he never got to see what the other inhabitants of Color Land had managed to see. The one constant that remains is the legend that had existed ever since, where it was written that as far as color is concerned, new and fresh possibilities will go on appearing endlessly.

FOUND AGAIN

Nearing sunset on a late afternoon, Death was in fact on his way to collect the last emperor of the magnificent and distinct civilization. Knowing this, the emperor was already pronouncing his last words, "My dear faithful people, I will soon be dying, but before I do, you must know this long withheld secret. The treasure, our real treasure was never stolen. It remains hidden in the heart of our very own land, in one of its many special corners. In order to save this treasure of ours, it has had to remain unseen even by you, but the time has come for you to know about it and hopefully recover it. When you find an unusual clay coffer with a golden eagle engraved on the center of its lid, you will recognize it as our long-buried treasure. Inside the coffer, you will find our most longed-for wealth that was never taken away. But you have to realize that since it has remained removed from our lives for many years, it will be hard for you to find out what it is, and why you have to take it back now. Meanwhile, until you have that happy opportunity, I wish that you lead your lives wisely, with dignity and honor." Those were the emperor's last words, and he died that same night, leaving his people with unsolved mystery. What was this treasure, and why was it so important?

In the emperor's land, there had been for the longest time much talk about a stolen treasure, but it was always addressed as one of those old legends that every human society likes to keep alive, because people like to gossip about something they wish were true. This is far from the same as really believing in the possibility of the actual existence of a treasure they could really find. Thinking they may have lost some magnificent stolen treasure, however, had often proved great consolation, carrying them through the many severe losses their kingdom, like all great kingdoms, had had to endure. It was therefore a bit of a shock to hear their last emperor declare there really had been a treasure all along, and that it had not been stolen. It was peculiar to consider it was now up to them to find it.

Because the idea of a stolen treasure had become such a pillar of their culture, people did not know how to relate to a treasure that had never been lost. It seemed rather weird simply to try to find it. In fact, it felt like a tradition had been stolen from them, one they could trust, and that this treasure, whatever it turned out to be, would be paltry in comparison. Some people grumbled that this unexpected information had been dropped in their laps by an emperor who was leaving them. Others were consumed by curiosity as to what the treasure would turn out to be. "It must be fine gold and silver of the sort our people were once so famous for," said one. "…embedded with precious stones they had gathered," said another. "Perhaps there are beautiful pearls, and corals, that reflect the perfection one could find in the ocean!" said a third, "…and so we can once more become rich!" said many others.

"So why shouldn't we go to find it?" wondered a young man who had been participating in the talk. "But where would we go look for it? Our land is too big!" said an older man. "We don't even know where to begin! We may get lost ourselves looking for the hidden treasure, since we don't even know what it is!" said someone else. "I think I would like to participate in this adventure. Even if we don't know what we may find, we can have a lot of fun!" said the youngest. On and on the talking went, as different ideas and feelings were poured into what had already begun to be the beginning of the search for the lost treasure.

Facing the remote possibility of a treasure to be found, there were some people who became really interested and started planning different strategies. Others kept wondering if finding "the treasure" could be at all possible, when for years and years it had remained lost. Typically, some people were unable to think there was a treasure at all. "It has only been a story we were always told," they said," and people nowadays are wanting to take every story as a fact, and this time, they are actually investing their time and energy in one that may very well be impossible."

The women who participated in this discussion provided conversation that was not so gray. Their comments were tinged with colors like intrigue, aliveness, hope, and belief, and they made the prospect of the search more fun. To be sure, the women did not know anything more than the men when it came to what could be said about the lost treasure, but when they talked, everyone could feel that talking about looking for the treasure was a conversation that had a reason. If the quality of their interest counted for anything, it was that it could lead to something, since no one really knew where the treasure could be—every idea regarding its totally unknown existence had to be considered. For the women, just talking seriously about what they're looking for might involve opening the transcendent importance of the search ahead. "It could really change our whole history," said one woman, "our children could be raised with a totally different idea about who they are based on where they come from, for they would finally know the secret of their great-great-grandparents, the people from whom they descend." As the women gathered, there rose from them a new voice that felt so confident and alive—it was contagious. The children in this town began paying close attention to what, not only their fathers, but their mothers were talking about. Out of a desire to participate in what had created so much interest in their parents, children began playing a new game of their own invention, which they called, "Let's find the lost Treasure."

As for attempts at actually finding the treasure rather quickly, every idea that people could think of was tried. With lack of results, however, the enthusiasm for the task began noticeably to decrease. The only ones who didn't seem to have gotten tired of the endless search were the children, who went on playing and having fun with the game they had made of finding the treasure. They designed a way to look for the treasure that met their needs, and so they always got to play when they searched, and the fun renewed their interest, their energy, bringing them close to each other even when they didn't actually bring anything concrete back home.

And so it happened that when most of the adult population was ready to give up, when even the men got tired of thinking, trying, and doing; when the women were also exhausted of the wishing and the praying and the talking, it was the children who, having fun with their play, went on with the adventure of finding the treasure. They in fact were the last ones of all people who needed to find any treasure, since for them, the treasure was their play itself, the fun they found from being and sharing with one another, and living a life distinct from the one attempted by the adults. The children's purpose was indeed fulfilled— they had found their treasure in having so much fun. They were happy, and their goal, which remained actually finding the lost unknown treasure they had heard so much about from their parents, was not more important to them than what they had already found.

Nothing good happens, however, without being noticed. One day, when some children were at play, a man that was walking by casually observed how totally engaged they were in the game they were playing. It moved him to see how easily these children were able to give themselves over to this activity. How happy they seemed to be! He was amazed that the children could take having fun so seriously. He realized he was himself far from used to taking up anything in his life in such a playful, naive, and happy manner. While wondering how the children managed to do this, he decided to carefully observe it, and resolved to walk by that same playground once each day in the course of fulfilling his adult duties.

The weather was good, and the walks always energized him. His observations, however, did not take him much farther in understanding the purpose of the game the children were playing. They spoke of a treasure, but he never saw any. One day, however, he watched the children playing with a clay coffer. "That certainly looks interesting," he thought to himself, as he approached closer to see what the children would do with what they had found. It didn't take him long to realize that the coffer with which the children were playing exactly matched the description the emperor had given of the box containing the treasure. It even seemed to have in the very center of its lid, the engraving of an eagle. At first he thought the children have fashioned their own replica. The craftsmanship was too fine, and too antique for this to be the case. "It can't be possible!" thought the man, "but could this actually be the coffer that has been keeping the treasure safe…?" A rush of blood appeared in his face, and his heart began to pound. There really wasn't any other explanation. They must have found the coffer the Emperor had told everyone about. As he watched for what the children would do next, he realized he would have to learn from them what they would do with a container that is likely to hold a very great treasure.

The Children in their play simply were trying to open the lid of the coffer. All sorts of ideas crossed through the man's mind, very quickly, as he went on observing, and they brought him less and less patience toward how the children went on casually playing. For instance, one of the children, the one who on that particular day had been nominated to play the king, commanded, "Now we are going to distribute the unopened treasure, everyone can keep a part of it while we play and will have to take care of that part, for at the end of the day, we will all be putting the treasure back together to hide it once again for tomorrow."

Exasperated, the man opened his eyes as big and wide as he possibly could in order to see what the children could possibly be pretending to divide among themselves. He knew already whatever they had in their minds could hardly represent the treasure that was still lying in the coffer they had not figured out how to open.

Then almost immediately, he recovered himself from the childishness of his adult annoyance and simply said to himself, "Children playing, nothing more than that! How could I ever have expected that there might be something more than them simply having fun, and anyway…" he did not get to finish his mental sentence because he was suddenly blinded by the intense reflection of the morning sunlight. "What's this?" he wondered. "Where is this coming from with such intensity? This isn't any sun I know." He realized he was staring at the coffer, and the reflection was coming from the gold engraving on the lid, which evidently had the power to intensify any light it reflected back. Looking at the lid once again, he became aware he was totally blinded. This time, he began trembling, not with fear but real excitement. "Could this be…? Is it…The Coffer? The real one?" He felt his heart strongly beating. "I have never felt such intensity," he thought. But as the man kept trying to figure out what was happening inside himself, he looked upon the coffer, which he was now sure, was the one that had been hidden for generations. The children went on with their play. Finally, just as their play king had asked them to do, each of the children put his or her share of the treasure back into the coffer, quite as if they had really opened it, and then went off to hide the coffer somewhere it would be hard to find. Practically paralyzed in awe, the man silently walked back home—a distance of several miles. Along the way, he came to realize that he needed some rest and resolved to come back the next day to the very same spot where he had seen the coffer with his very own eyes, that is until the intensity of the light flashing back from it had rendered him blind.

It was a very long night for the man. What he had witnessed left him incredulous in a state of mixed awe and misunderstanding. When the sun finally came out and the new day began, he was delighted to be done with the effort to go to sleep. He was not at all tired. He could hardly wait to go back and observe the children playing, hoping he would soon see the strange coffer with which they had found the day before. So confident was he that the children would find it again that he called some friends to join him to observe what had left him so very impressed. When he and a few friends arrived at the playground—where the children were already playing and had indeed found and were once again unable to open the coffer—the children did not scatter at their approach. The men asked, "We see you cannot open that coffer. Let us take a look." The children welcomed them to do so. So the men approached closer.

As the men got their chance to look directly at the lid of the coffer, despite the careful description their friend had already given them, they were totally surprised that they could see on the coffer's lid a gold engraving of an eagle that matched exactly the description their king had given them the previous year. Observing what they had all long been looking for, they could no longer restrain their desire to hold the coffer in their own hands. Once they had lifted it up, one of the men eagerly asked, "Do you want us to help? Let's help you see what your coffer contains?" The children, hesitating, answered, "We found this coffer while we were playing by some of the rocks, but we have not been able to open it, it is too hard, and…" but the child was interrupted by the men's anxiety to see what was inside, and at that moment one of the men took hold of the coffer decisively and said, "Let me open it up for you, we need to see what's inside." This time, the children had no time to answer since the anxious hands of the man had commanded the coffer. He had even brought special tools to do the work that was required to open the lid that had been sealed for many years.

The man worked for some time in opening the coffer, and before he was through, his partners had to help. By then, more people arrived—together with the children and the group of men, they all gathered to observe what was taking place at the public playground. After waiting for so many years, everyone present wanted to witness the opening of the coffer. Facing such a dramatic moment, the first ones who were able to say something when they all could look into the opened coffer were the children. "Feathers, they are feathers!!" exclaimed one of them. "Oh this is fabulous!" cried a second child. "They have all those beautiful colors!" said a third, adding, "aren't we lucky!"

The men who had worked so hard to open the lid had a totally different reaction. "Feathers? Is that It? Only feathers? How can this be?

This coffer matches exactly the description our emperor gave of the one holding the treasure, but how could he think of feathers as treasure? Did he know that's what the coffer contained? Who would think of feathers as treasure?" wondered the men. "And what in the world are we supposed to do with this bunch of useless feathers?" said someone else. "Why is this a gift? This is not fair, this is not a treasure!" Then one of the oldest men, who until then had kept quiet in the midst of such perplexity, intervened.

"Perhaps we can ask the birds, they have feathers, don't they? And they have knowledge we have forgotten or perhaps have never known. Hopefully they can help us decipher what this treasure is about."

They decided to go ask help from the birdman, a wise man who long ago had been able to communicate with the birds. A large group of people went to see him, all interested in finding out what he would do with such an unexpected treasure as feathers. When they arrived, they asked the birdman if he could find out from the birds the kind of treasure feathers hold. The birdman who had for years been observing and studying birds, and long ago had found his personal treasure in the relationship that had come into being between him and members of the Bird Kingdom, was quite willing to ask his bird friends about the kind of feathers these people were totally unable to appreciate.

He agreed to help on condition that the birds themselves would be willing to participate in supplying what the people needed. Of course, observing the feathers, he immediately recognized that they mainly belonged to the *Quetzal*. As a consequence, he kept his eyes on the sky, and sure enough, that bird, whose feathers constituted such a large part of the content of the coffer, made its appearance. When seeing this gorgeous bird fly by, the birdman began calling him through different movements and sounds. The bird indeed came closer and stood up on the branch of the very same tree that was offering its shade to the group of men who had come to find out what possible treasure they had actually found. Finally, the birdman offered the wisdom he had received from communicating with the *Quetzal*. "Whoever sees, touches, or wears *Quetzal* feathers is always reminded of the beauty in nature." Still unable to understand, the men asked again. "Why is that a treasure?" "Nature herself is a treasure," said the birdman, "and a big part of that is her beauty—being able to perceive it is a precious gift that very few people ever get to receive."

Was this supposed to be an answer? The men kept quietly looking at each other. Clearly unsatisfied with what they were told, one of them finally said, "Excuse me for insisting, Birdman, but could you ask some other bird from one of the many species that cross the sky the same question, so we can hear another opinion?" The birdman was sensitive enough to understand that such an answer, even if offered by birds of another species, would not meet the men's expectation. So he thought for a while and then he said, "If we are able to see an eagle, the very same eagle whose golden engraving appears on the lid of the coffer, I will call out to that eagle. He travels around the world, I think his wisdom might help."

It took a couple of days before the birdman saw high enough in the sky a flying eagle. When the bird started to fly lower and closer, the birdman openly called to him saying, "Excuse me for interrupting your beautiful flight, Eagle, but there is a question I would like to ask you. Would you have some time for a conversation?" The eagle descended even closer, close enough to be able to hear the birdman's follow-up request. "From your wide-ranging knowledge, could you please tell me what feathers are for?" The eagle, feeling the respect with which an old friend had approached him, responded with a fulsome account. "Feathers are what cover our body. Our feathers protect us, being at the same time practically weightless, they never impede flying and moving around. May I know why you have asked this question?"

The group of people gathered, aided by the birdman, began to answer for him. "We found this treasure which consists of feathers. We don't want to offend you but we do not understand how feathers can be a treasure." The eagle turned his head to look at them. "Do you think you would ever be able to fly and see the grandeur of the world with its many possibilities if you would wear them?" asked the eagle. "Never," answered the people. "We are too heavy to fly, our structure is too dense to be able to fly, we admire how you can do it with your feathers but that freedom was not granted to us human beings and these feathers won't make that possible." "Well," said the eagle, "I am not of your opinion. I think of feathers as being a treasure for anyone who wears them. Isn't there something in you that already knows it can fly?" The birdman realized the people who had gathered were now at a loss, so he went on pressing the eagle. "Maybe because we are people and not birds, we don't seem to see anything in us that could fly. I like to think that we have not yet found the reason to do so. Perhaps you could help by telling us what gets you to fly?" For this question, the eagle had a most natural answer. "When I fly, I get to see the world from many different angles, I see it under different shades of light, various intensities, I get to find different corners, yet unseen and unknown by many. No matter how high I go, I am always keeping an eye on earth, where I also belong." He continued, "you see, when flying up high, all the narrowness that one gets to feel when you stand in one sole place suddenly expands, the world seems wider and richer, I get to see new views of the very same spot I had found myself thinking was narrow for me. It is through flying that my narrowness and the sudden expansion empowers me. Then I am able to act." The eagle paused for a moment and then he said, "I must say I feel very sorry for anyone who can't fly in any possible way. That seems to be a very poor life, always proceeding by standing, and always having to do so in some place where you only have that immediate view of life. But perhaps, now that you humans have found your treasure, it will help you fly." After finishing what he had to say, the eagle left flying in the sky showing his grandeur.

As the eagle departed, the men who were present thanked the birdman for his honest try at helping decipher the incomprehensible treasure. They left his house in awe, pondering the words of the eagle. "What in us can fly…and perhaps bring us out of our immediate view of life…?" They had never heard of anyone in the human realm being able to fly. However, they remembered how their great-great-grandparents used to wear interwoven feathers as a type of crest over their heads, which was called the *Penachos*. Beautifully ornamented, this constituted a most precious attire. It was worn over people's head only on special occasions, and its feathers, among that population, had been so deeply valued, always selecting the very best and most beautiful ones for the emperor's *Penacho*.

"Memories, only memories!" said one of the men in the group, "and all from the same story of deceit and abuse that caused us to lose our treasure in the first place!" He was right, of course, and the people felt the pain of loss as they wondered what they could do now with the treasure they had found. It seemed to belong to another time that could never return. And as the men kept spinning around the longing they had always associated with the treasure, trying to deal with the poverty of being unable to fly, even with feathers at hand, their energy began sinking and their sorrow became more and more dense.

In the meantime, the children who had found the clay coffer in the first place believing they had really found a treasure were playing different kinds of game with it to celebrate. On and on went the children enjoying themselves as they created new ways to interact with their world including the newly found feathers. They were able to assign all sorts of amusing meanings to the feathers, and these new meanings were incorporated into their joy of sharing in the old source the fun they had found.

There was almost an abyss between the approach of this group of children and the group of adults who had gathered later in relation to the treasure that had been found. While contemplating the feathers, the children felt lighter, lifted by their imagination and illuminated by the amplitude of their sight totally beyond their previous customary play. The adults, watching the children with incomprehension, were in the midst of darkness and immobility.

Anyone observing the children at play, though, would have had to wonder, if perhaps it was the feathers themselves, which the children had quickly taken to holding really tight against their bodies, even if not in the *penacho* style of the glorious past that had made such a flight of imagination possible. The children were now open to a wide and abundant view of endless possibilities that empowered them in their aliveness. By contrast, the adults were not willing to try, certainly not wear any of the despised feathers, and not surprisingly, they could not resist the gravity of their own ideas and old beliefs. All they knew was that they were unable to fly in the sky, as indeed no human can do. More limiting was that they were not able to find the lightness they needed to move across the very same earth on which they were left to stand. It would occur to anyone watching this group of men, that there are those who even, when holding a treasure in their very own hands, will never be able to recognize it. The group of men lost perspective in realizing that they were the ones trusted with the major of all secrets, one that in order to be saved, had to remain hidden for years and years as if lost. Men in their disappointment lost sight of being the heirs of a long buried wisdom. One could even get to think that there are people who, no matter what they find, again and again, will keep closed the wings of their imagination. They are never to know the amplitude of an eagle's view, and so they will never find the beauty of the *Quetzal*.

Even among the unimaginative men, however, struggling to figure out what had delighted the children about the treasure of a few sacred feathers, ideas began to fly, ideas that were very much like flying feathers. That didn't help anyone actually to fly, but perhaps one day, that deep knowledge that there is a treasure still to be discovered in the feathers of the *Quetzal* will allow some men to get past the certainty with which they live their earthbound lives, and maybe those few will achieve some perspective from above onto their view of life. When that will take place, we can be sure the hidden treasure will be found again.

TOLD STORY

Surrounded by wide, round-topped mountains was a small old valley, which had been admired by almost anybody who came to visit, because for years, beautiful flowers had been growing there. Rare species of all kinds of flowers had found a home in this place. The most exquisite colors, shapes, and perfumes embraced the scenery, creating a sensual atmosphere. The small valley, which had long been a most enjoyable place to visit, went by the name of Flower Valley. Midsize mountains protected the place from strong winds and changes in temperature, so that it had year round a temperate micro-climate, and there was also a river that crossed the valley right through its middle, enabling the soil to stay fresh and moist. It had become one of those special places on the earth where life can flourish and evolve.

Flowers seemed to like the conditions given by nature in this small corner of the world, and by now, generations of beautiful flowers had come into being benefiting from the favorable circumstances. People who were lucky enough to live close by would often come to this valley to take long walks, and those who did always commented on how much they enjoyed witnessing the ever-evolving beauty. Nature had bestowed a blessing they were able to witness and its splendor made everyone lucky enough to enjoy and willing to assist in the preservation of such beauty. As a consequence, people, without being asked, would help with trimming of branches, weeding, and sweeping the leaves that had fallen across the moist ground. Some people even took it upon themselves to fertilize the flowers that needed extra nurturing. In this way, people who loved the valley assured that it stayed fertile.

Water, the one indispensable element for any living being to survive, had never been a worry since this part of the world enjoyed an adequate rainfall. The rain provided plenty of water, not only for the flowers, but also to replenish the river.

Years passed by without any interruption in this privileged natural miracle, until one day, for some unknown reason, the rain stopped falling so often. In fact, for several weeks in a row, it didn't fall at all. At first, this didn't seem so great a problem. The days were still beautiful, and only the river itself seemed narrower, as well it should have, since there was indeed less water running in its riverbed. The flowers were still in bloom. But after a while they too began to show the strain of losing their precious liquid nourishment. They began looking somehow pale, and they lost the brightness in the colors that had always characterized them. Now it was clear that the valley was really suffering from its rain-less condition. People had hoped that rain would return to allow the river to fill up again, and for the soil around the flowers to recover its moistness. This hope seemed in vain after days had passed and the land became more and more dry.

Among the flowers facing this situation, and trying gamely to proud-ly hold their heads up, there were ones in bloom that seemed okay from the outside and a few that had fainted from excessive thirst, but even so, they appeared to hold up pretty well. But there were also delicate ones who had only recently bloomed, and they did not look as if their confidence could possibly last. In this way, more and more, the once beautiful and inspiring Flower Valley began to look sad and in danger.

Into this now unhappy place, one early morning at dawn, as she had done since the beginning of time, the Fairy of all Flowers arrived. She had come to do her usual rounds through all the different flowerbeds. As was her custom, she had brought with her the dew to spray, which, hov-ering above the flowers, she would disperse to assure the continuity of their gorgeous brilliance. As she approached her Valley, for she regarded it as her special preserve, she sadly became aware of the difficulty the flowers were going through. She came especially near and asked them, "Oh, my dear ones, what can be going on here? How can it be that you look so very weak and frightened?" The flowers that were still strong enough, felt happy to talk to the Flower Fairy wanting to answer in the affirmative, but they could not. They heard themselves saying with dismay, "We have no water to drink, and it has been already a very long time that we have had to survive under this very hard condition." Sev-eral flowers were even more direct. "We have been trying to survive as best as we possibly can, but we are so very thirsty." A particular flower said, "We don't know when the water we still have will run out." After that outburst, more desperate voices sounded. "I am afraid the time of water will very soon be over, it could become necessary for all of us to learn to live without any water." This idea created panic, and other voices among the flowers spoke to the anxious flower who had made such a terrible suggestion, "how dare you say such a thing, how could we flowers survive without water, we would be sure to die." "Perhaps," said an elder flower, "we have to ration the water we still have, and we have to learn to live with the least possible amount. We need to save water now for when even worse times arrive!" "Worse times?" chimed in some of the younger flowers, who did not respect their elders. "What do you mean by that? There can't be anything worse than this. If we stop drinking the little water we still have, we are for sure going die. So much for rationing!" To this, the elder flower said again, "We have to learn to live with the least possible amount of water." But for making that wise statement she also got an impertinent answer. "You can say that because you are old and have at most a few more days to live. I on the other hand have baby buds which all need water now!"

On and on went the laments of the flowers raising their voices, which had never before been heard in the valley, addressing the Fairy of all Flowers, as if she had never considered their situation. The Flower Fairy was the only one able to hear them, but she had the heart to do so, and she became aware of the great suffering the rain-free weeks in the valley had caused. It hurt her terribly to see her beloved flowers drooping, and to hear their anguished remarks. She bent her head down for a moment to think. What could she do to help the flowers under her care? At last she spoke, in a careful, crystalline voice, "I so wish I could bring the water you are in such desperate need of, but that is not in my realm of responsibility and thus not in my power to do. I do not even know why you have to go through this terrible dry spell. What it is in my power to offer is what I hope you are all feeling now. Every day at dawn, you will have the moist touch of my dew, and that will open up a voice in each of you that anyone will be able to hear. Just as what took place this morning, you will be able to express your innermost feelings." Hearing this, the flowers were far from reassured. "But who will be able to hear our voices as they cry out our needs?" they asked. "Who would ever be willing to hear what a flower has to say? And who would believe what we say really comes from us?" The Fairy of all Flowers bent her head down again, and then she gave her answer, "Anybody who is really interested, any of those who can feel the passion for nature and beauty that you show every day, any of those who care for life in all its manifestations, any of those will have no trouble hearing you and knowing that the voices you raise could only come from you." "Trust me," continued the fairy, "every morning when the first rays of sun will appear in the sky, if my dew gives you voices, those voices will be heard by the people who have always valued your presence." And having said that in her firm, grave, crystalline voice, she left the flowers in her beloved valley and went off, flowing with the wind, to go on spraying all the flowers in the world with her empowering dew.

For the rest of that day, the flowers remained still, savoring the fairy's gift. The moist dew she had brought that morning, accompanied by her promise to return, made them feel a bit stronger even though they were still facing dryness in their lives they had never known before. Their fairy had planted in their hearts the hope they needed to endure this precarious moment in the long story of their existence in the valley.

Time passed by and the water condition did not improve. There was no rain. The unfed river, growing thinner, had less and less to offer to the valley floor. People who would so much enjoy walking among all the different flowers were deeply concerned with what had become a desperate prospect. Soon, all the flowers would die. The morning dew was not enough to overturn their doom. The people knew they had to intervene. In order to save the flowers that remained, already drooping their heads as if in a final sleep, each person who didn't want that outcome would have to show their interest in keeping the flowers alive now. In practical human terms, this meant that flowers were going to be transplanted and taken to a different location, where they could be watered and specially nurtured until their color and vitality returned.

Many people were happy to do this, although they worried that it might already be too late.

Soon came the day assigned to take this drastic measure. Early that morning, among the people who arrived at the valley was a woman holding a flowerpot in order to take some flowers home where she could care for them. As she walked through the corridors made of still-growing flowers, the woman saw some of the buds that had just appeared into life, struggling to burst into bloom out of the hopelessly dry soil. As she saw them, the woman immediately knew that those buds held the future of the flowers she wanted to care for, and so with utmost caution, she dug into the earth. As she was taking the budding plants out of the dry ground, she kept hearing voices—for there seemed to be many more than one—saying, "I am afraid! And so am I. And me too." "I must be dreaming," thought the woman. "I have been so worried for these flowers that now I even think I am hearing their voices!" "Nevertheless," she said, "they are right to trust me, I will take good care of them, and in my care they will be fine." The woman said this aloud, thinking she was talking only to herself.

When she arrived home, she looked around for the best places to put the flowering plants she had taken from the valley, where it would not be too hot or too airy, not too dark and not too excessively sunny; places where they could get the best possible light and temperature. The woman accommodated each flowering plant as meticulously as she was able, wanting the flowers to experience her place as their home. She started by pouring fresh water into each pot, to give every dry root system its chance to recover. She then went on with her usual house chores until late that afternoon, when she came back to see how the flowers were doing. To her surprise, she found that almost all the water that she had poured that morning into the various flower pots was still there—untouched. The buds had not taken up hardly any of the water. "Oh!" she exclaimed, "how come you have not drunk any water? I thought that was what flowers like the most! And certainly it's what you most need! There has been such a lack of water at the valley so long that you were almost about to die. I wonder why you still can't accept living water." There was no answer. The evening wore on, and tired from the long day of trying to save the flowers, the woman went to bed. She had not lost hope, and was ready to wake up in the morning to find what the new day would bring.

It was very early in the morning, so early that the very first rays of light were just appearing in the sky when the woman woke up. She ran to see the buds, and was amazed to behold that practically all the water that she poured the day before was still there. Only a hard to perceive amount was missing. The good-hearted woman found this unbelievable. Sitting down in front of the flowerpots and with an impotent voice she asked, "Why aren't you drinking water? I just can't understand why you're not…"

Just as the Flower Fairy had promised, the flowers she was trying to water were able to talk, and the woman did get an answer, "We prefer not to drink water." With wide-open eyes, the woman said, "Am I hearing voices? Or is there really someone talking?" "Yes," answered the buds." "*We* are." "Excuse me," said the woman, "Who is this *we*? I can't see anybody but these lovely, sad buds." "Yes, that is right, you are seeing us, we are the ones talking to you and it is we who are saying that we prefer not to drink water." Hard as it was to believe, the voices were coming from the buds. So the woman said, "This sure is one more surprise for coming to see you so very early in the morning. Well, since we can have a talk, may I ask why you prefer not to drink water?"

"It's just that we don't feel like drinking," said a voice. "We don't really like it that much," said another one of the buds at the flowerpot. "Why should we need so much water, it is okay if we don't drink, we will be fine," said a third one. The woman, astonished, couldn't imagine how to argue with this, so she kept quietly observing the new odd buds that were so sure they could live without water.

A few days later, with the buds still alive, the woman confirmed that they were indeed able to talk at dawn. She also got more of an explanation for the perverse behavior she was sure was going to kill them. That early morning, one of the buds said to her, "where we come from, there was very little water, it has been so since we were born, flowers around us have gone through much fear as they sensed that soon there won't be any water left; and we have heard our mother expressing pain because our flowers will have to face the uncertainty of the future that this lack of water will bring. Her fear has been so great that it brought terrible suffering to us, for we often heard her cry!"

Another of the buds opened its mouth to say, "Most probably we did something wrong, I think we misbehaved because we were so thirsty. Probably we wanted to drink too much water when there was none, and so we took water that our parents needed. My guess is that this is why they were suffering!" A third bud said, "You must be right, I also used to hear our mother often crying, and I too thought to myself, if we wouldn't have been so mean, drinking the water, perhaps then she would have had a drink and been able to caress us with her petals. They were so soft and moist you know, enough to make us feel humid and happy. I am sure we misbehaved with so much selfish drinking, it became impossible for her to do so too!" Another bud said, "Our great-grandmother used to say that drinking up all the wanted water was not having good manners, she told us always to remember, 'The least the better, then you will be safe,' she told us to remember this at all times." Last of all, a new bud added, "I think I don't even like drinking water, at times water makes me sick, so I have decided to take each day a little less, as our great-grandmother told us to do. If she were here, she would be proud of me."

Hearing suddenly all these voices told her why the buds were no longer drinking water, the good-hearted woman heard herself inwardly crying. She, who since that very first day when she had brought the buds to her own home to save them and had been wondering why the buds were drinking hardly any water, was finally being told by the buds themselves the story they had been told by their grandparents, which explained so much. She remained quiet, and as well as she knew that the buds were not going to survive without water, she also understood that the buds were trying to honor something that was as important to their continuity as life itself.

The woman did not question again the buds' reason for not drinking water, for she had heard the told story by which the buds had always lived. It was clear that the buds could not drink their fill of water, and she did not insist that they do so. With deep feelings of compassion for the suffering buds, one day at dawn, as if she herself had been sprayed with a fresh mist, some thoughts began flowing from her moistened heart, "What is it that we live for, if not the unimaginable? I have surely learned that much from these buds…the surprise every day brings! Many things happen which no one has even dreamed about until they do. That has to mean that life is what takes place no matter what other people, or we ourselves think, wish for, and expect. Who would have thought, for instance that in the most exquisite Valley of Flowers the lives of these buds would be tested by such dryness as the one that took place? And who could have ever imagined that the buds would take on the suffering of remaining dry? And, most of all, who would have imagined that I would ever hear their voices?"

Flowing with these moist ideas, the woman decided she would share her reverie with the buds. She had always loved singing, so one morning after she had woken up right before dawn, she walked into the kitchen and prepared herself a hot tea into which she poured some honey. As she slowly drank her tea, she went walking close by the buds and softly began to sing. She sang what she loved—songs composed out of what for her, were deeply meaningful poems. Singing such songs made her feel joyful as she circled the buds, knowing she was going around the core essence of their beings, caressing them with her soft and musical voice. The buds stayed quiet until she finished. Then there was silence. The woman spoke in her usual voice, "That was for you, it is called singing, I enjoy it so very much. I wanted to share it with you."

After that, the woman went on singing every morning. This ritual became how she started her day. One morning, while an especially clear and beautiful blue sky was beginning to appear, she extended an invitation to the buds to sing along with her. "To sing?" asked the buds amazed, "but we are buds, and buds only, we don't know how to sing." "Ah, but I thought you had found your voices, I thought I could help you train them as I have trained mine. For that reason, I thought you might want to try singing. But it can be simpler than that. If you feel like it you can join me any time." Curious, one of the buds asked, "What is it that you drink before singing to get such a soft pure voice?" "It is honey, which is good for your throat, and especially good for singing. Let me offer each of you a drop." "Do we have throats?" asked another bud who had been listening intently. "I cannot be sure you do," answered the woman, "yet you must because you have a voice! It might be good for your individual voices to be softened by honey, and anyway it is sweet and delicious!" So this time she put some drops of honey into the little bit of water that she usually put into the buds' soil, saying as she did so, "Please enjoy this when you feel like it. I have plenty, and I love its presence in my life."

It was awhile before the buds dared to try what seemed to them almost too human, and certainly unknown, and far from natural for them to be able to do, but nevertheless, one unexpected morning they began to sing along with the woman as she carried out her daily ritual. The woman knew immediately that other voices had joined her singing. Even though she felt deep joy in her heart, she did not say a word. She was so happy that the buds had discovered singing. Their voices added to her own became a choir sharing a rare and marvelous opportunity.

The buds and the woman began living a new story that was their own creation. It told of being introduced to a world of compassion, sweetness, and joy. But its newness also brought consequence to the old story by which flowers had always lived—the buds became thirsty. Unnoticeable at the very beginning before this change, the time came when they became aware of the increased amount of water they are now consuming.

It was just at that point, when happy times seemed finally to have arrived, that something totally unpredictable once again took place— the buds stopped singing and refused to absorb any water at all. They seemed to have retracted their willingness to ease their own path toward bloom, as if they had gotten scared. In fact they were scared, scared of abandoning their very first told story, which had always insisted on being kept present and alive. Their daring attempt of foregoing their restriction of water intake so as to include some honey in their lives had provoked a severe reaction, one that once again seemed to be leading them to the very same death they were on the brink of before. The woman noticed this severe reaction appeared just as the buds were beginning to come alive again. That morning, the only thing she could hear were the buds recounting the told story passed on to them by their mother, grandmother, and great-grandmother, about the wrongness of drinking too much water. The old told story was once again alive, furiously claiming its hearers to enliven its only truth.

Under this pressure to respect the tradition of the past, the new vision of accepting the thirst of life, and any possibility of the buds becoming fresh and humid was simply erased from their reality. The told story had resumed command, with all its power to refuse moistness and flow.

Witnessing how the old told story took over the buds' existence as their voices repeated it, the woman was disturbed. This reaction was so violent, and so total! All she could do to calm herself was to resume her own singing. She now realized, that as much as she had honestly wanted to assist the buds, she had never really incorporated the buds' own story into her own, soft, honeyed singing. Instead, she had gone with only what was meaningful to her. The buds' told story had felt absurd and lifeless to her. Nevertheless, it was and had been their only story. She had to admit she had never recognized it. This realization made her suddenly feel very far indeed from the real life of her dear buds and farther still from their honest survival attempt, which had led them to join her in her singing. The woman realized her lack of sensitivity and awareness. She had failed to include consideration in her saving attitude.

Filled with compassion for the buds, and with self-forgiving shame at her own blindness, she decided to write a new song. She had been singing for a long time, but tonight, she wanted to write a song into which she could bring the sadness she felt at having ignored the long told story that was the buds' very religion. In the song she created out of the fullness of her compassion for them, for their Valley, and for herself, she celebrated years they had been blessed with an abundance of moist soil. There, told her song, hundreds of flowers were able to grow under privileged conditions, and every morning, even in the worst times of dryness, there was still moistening dew. The woman's song expressed the larger vision that included the old told story, but was not restricted to it. As she started to sing the song she had now created, she became aware of the difficulty inherent in any such endeavor, for no one can incorporate every element that should be there into one inclusive song for everyone to live by. Knowing this made her feel really close to the buds.

Finally, she was ready to share her new composition with the buds. As she sang to them, she realized that this song was the first she had ever written herself. When her singing was over, there was a wonderful silence. The buds were speechless. They had realized that their endless repetition of their old told story could stop. Eventually, they were able to communicate once again to the woman. "You are singing our story... we thought it was not important...to anyone...until today."

The song had reminded the buds of the Flower Fairy, and for the first time, they spoke to the woman about her. "She arrives every morning at dawn..." the buds said, "riding on one of the sun's first rays of light." "Have you seen her?" asked the woman, who was intrigued by this image "I don't know what you mean by seeing her," answered one of the buds, "but we do feel her, we have her moistness in us, every day." That revelation led the woman to realize that the Flower Fairy had always been present in the buds' lives at all times. She learned that it was not only the soil's humidity, but also the sky's different moistness that had enabled the buds to survive and to go on living. It was then that a new told story began, one able to incorporate in itself the old story, but adding to it a humanized possibility of living the entirety of what gave the buds existence. Without really being aware how they did it, or when, the buds began singing once again. Their new old song made them thirsty for life's essential moistness. Only now, the new song did not forget the old told story, for it said:

> *Thank you for reminding me,*
> *Considering all other times in life,*
> *Even those that long ago were true;*
>
> *I now know how precious water is*
> *I also know it can be missing at any time,*
> *And I can be scared to death when that happens,*
> *As I have already been before,*
> *But today there is water, and I will be drinking it.*
> *Thank you for reminding me to take care*
> *As drinking water is also caring.*

The buds kept on singing this song as if chanting, and soon, something else began to take place. They began to swell. "Do you think we are drinking too much water?" they would from time to time ask the woman, and each time the woman would respond, "Oh, well, I don't really think so, this is called growing, now you are bigger." Soon after, spring arrived and in some of the buds a very tiny orange blossom began to be seen. The woman who by now was sensitive enough to know the buds, knew that when any change took place, she would be asked the same worrying question, "Is this the result of drinking water? Perhaps now it is indeed too much?" And she would have to go on carefully answering with new songs that were recurrently needed for her dear buds to grow into blossoms. These songs always incorporated the old told story with the present living one—the ancient with the now, cohabiting in the woman's music. She learned to love composing as she witnessed how the chanting allowed the buds to go on with their lives and actually bloom. Little did she realize that she herself had come to flourish through her genuine and compassionate interest in life. As for the buds, they gratefully acknowledged the fact that their told story could be part of the story of the perfumed orange blossom they were able to proudly hold. This was the moist aliveness they were finally able to achieve.

COURAGEOUS HEART

The story that you are about to hear is told in the god's realm as well as among humans. Since these are usually thought of as clearly divided territories, it may surprise you that the gods tell each other stories just as we do. And let me add that regardless of human advances and knowledge, such as our understanding of embryology, physiology, and all the technology that has made medical science so successful in prolonging lives, the gods make sure to get together in order to assure that life among humans also continues. Each and every one of the gods will participate in a way that accords with his or her specific nature, for each has something different to offer to the task of creating new life in the human realm.

There are specific gods in charge of the craftsmanship of each of the parts needed to constitute a new being. Since each god has a different workshop in which to create his or her part of what it takes for new human babies to be born, the gods need time to come together to assemble what they have fashioned. They have already taken care of every little detail needed to fulfill their individual tasks, but above all, the assembly is in charge of infusing aliveness in each and every one of the parts that has been built.

The last of the parts to be added to the whole in the delicate work of assembly is the heart. When the rest of the pieces have been readied, this queen of the organs, the heart, is inserted lovingly into the body to enliven the person-to-be. The heart connects all the pieces in the assembly by allowing a warm and soft flow of living energy to circulate, creating then a unity of what constitutes the new baby-to-be. Humans might think, it is nothing but rushing blood, running around the now connected-together body. Yet, though the energy uses this channel, like all the others one can find in an assembled body, it is much, much more than blood. The gods call it energy, a mysterious force only they understand.

It was on one of these particular times of creation that this story begins. The gods had gathered in order to fulfill their creative task, when one of the hearts that had just begun palpitating and was ready to be delivered into the baby so that it could be born, had arrived looking particularly beautiful. Pink in shade, the heart had a special glow emanating from its very core. None of the gods could deny that it was alive. It took a brief moment of the precious assembly time for the goddess who had made that heart to enjoy the special beauty of the new little heart that was now infused with life. As she stared at it, its delivery was dangerously delayed. Hurrying to catch up, the goddess made sure the pink little heart got into the new body, but it arrived so quickly into the assembly that it turned out to be connected the other way around, the opposite of the way that was needed for a smooth, warm, and alive flow. The goddess was immediately aware of what had happened, and realized that if it stayed that way the new baby would turn blue, which would be a great problem, for that was a color that humans didn't understand. Thinking how enjoyable this little heart could be in a new life, if only it could still be connected properly, she immediately summoned a couple of angels. To them she said, "There is a baby on earth that is being born right now who really needs your help. It is my fault, for I was so very dearly enjoying the beauty of the little heart I had fashioned, that it arrived too late to be inserted properly, and it happened to be done on the opposite side. As you know, I can't go to earth myself, so I want to ask you to help me fix what was much too rapidly done."

While this conversation was going on in the gods' realm, a new baby girl was being born on earth. The happy mother and father were already embracing what they believed was their own creation. The new mother, looking with love at her newborn baby, was sure that she was the first to lay eyes on such precious a treasure. As is the case with every new mother, she could not imagine that her new baby had already been admired and enjoyed.

In the meantime, the two angels that would be coming to earth had planned with the goddess their intervention. The little heart needed to be repositioned in the baby's body in order for the baby to remain pink and healthy. The angels' plan was to ask the mother to lend them her baby for a little while. That idea might have worked in the realm of gods, but of course it could not work in the human realm since the new mother on earth would not allow anyone to take her baby away from her. The angels realized this as soon as they arrived on earth. Wondering how they could fulfill their task, they began to worry. One of the angels said, "There is no time left, the baby is turning blue, we have to save its little pink heart."

"I am not sure how we are going to do it," said the second angel. "The new mother will not allow the baby to be taken away from her for any reason."

"Oh, I can understand that," said the first angel. "It is a gorgeous baby, even the goddess herself kept enjoying and embracing her! I think…I think…that we are going to need to ask some help from Rainbow."

"From Rainbow?" asked the second angel. "How is Rainbow going to help us?" But by the time the second angel had thought to ask this, they had already arrived to see Rainbow, in that special corner in the sky where light keeps shining at all times.

The angel said, "Good morning, or good evening Rainbow. We are here in need of your help." "Hello friends," answered Rainbow. "How can I help you? Is it already raining? I have been so busy polishing the colors that I have not noticed any rain yet."

"Oh no Rainbow, this is something else, we want to ask you if you can take away all your colors from the earth, though of course only for a short period of time. We do not wish to offend you, colors are beautiful, but we need everything to be black for a while, only for a while. We ask this enormous favor because we need to fix an assembly that was done in a rush with a little pink heart that was intended to complete a newborn baby. It was connected the other way around and is making the newborn baby turn blue. Naturally, its mother won't let her baby be taken away from her, so we need a lot of black to do the necessary work."

"Well," said Rainbow, "you know how much I love colors, colors are my life, but I take your point…so let's see…well, I also love children, you know, actually they have always been the ones that most believe in what rainbows can do! They observe and enjoy me the longest, and while they are doing that, I get to hear the wishes they make. Perhaps this new baby is already wishing for something." "Sorry, Rainbow," interrupted the first angel. "We simply have no time to let you wait for this baby's first wish. This is an emergency! And the adults are in control. You know how human adults function, usually they have no time…" "Oh, yes, now I understand," said Rainbow. "You have asked me for something I do not have the heart to refuse. If it will help save this baby, I will let everything be Black!" As soon as all the colors heard Rainbow, they began packing themselves so that they could be carried off to a concealed place. At first, all they understood was that they were to take some vacations. So all the colors on earth happily packed up and waited until finally, Black arrived. And at that point, for all any human could see, there was only Black.

On earth, Mommy, Daddy, grandparents and a bunch of other people who had gathered to celebrate the new baby's arrival had started to worry and broke out crying when the baby began to turn blue.

"Why are they all suddenly crying?" asked the second angel. "We are already here to help! Because Rainbow left and took away all the colors, so now they can't see anything but black, the only hue remaining. They have lost sight of the future. Humans are like that," said the first angel. "They usually only believe in what they can see right now."

"It must be hard to be human," answered the second angel. "If they don't believe in anything other than what they are capable of physically seeing in the present, they certainly must be very near-sighted, almost forgetfully so…"

"Please pay attention," said the first angel. "We have to get moving now that Black has arrived. We have just enough secrecy to do our task, and we don't have time to penetrate the mystery of what it is to be human. We mustn't forget that the little pink heart is waiting!"

Ready to begin working, the angels announced to the gods that the time has come to fulfill the task that the goddess had assigned. Because even for the gods, everything was now black, and no one really saw how it took place. What gives life to anything has to remain a mystery. The little pink heart was somehow disconnected from the baby's body, and then carefully reassembled in order to allow the full flow of vibrant life begin to circulate throughout the newborn's recently created body. While this delicate procedure was taking place, the goddess herself was the one to safely preserve both the heart and the body of the baby. She was well aware that for a moment, the little one's body needed to survive without its heart, and that the little pink heart would have to beat outside of its assigned body. As brief as this time of separation was, it still placed a great demand on both parts of the baby, to have to stay alive without the other. The angels worked in a masterlike way, with upmost care and efficiency, but for the heart and the body they were working on, being apart from each other seemed to last for a terribly long time. Nevertheless, soon enough, the little pink heart was finally beating inside the baby's body, and the two, body and heart, found themselves reunited better than before.

Once this happened, the cold blue color in the baby's body began fading away and very slowly was replaced by a pale, emerging pink. It was obvious that life was now properly flowing. Black who had been totally present when so much needed was now permitted to leave, but he did so gradually. Eventually, he had left a space for Rainbow to unpack all the magnificent colors. Mommy, who had been desperately longing for her baby to come into the possibilities of life, could now see the living color of her beautiful baby.

Even though everyone on earth seemed to be enjoying the light and its brightness, nevertheless, the two angels lingered on earth to keep guard over the precious aliveness of the now successfully reassembled baby. To be honest, both angels were admiring the baby.

"What a beautiful baby this turned out to be," said the second angel. "Don't you think so?"

"Yes, she is gorgeous!" answered the first angel. "Aren't we lucky to have been the ones trusted to take care of her?"

"That is what every angel thinks," said the second angel.

"What do they always think?" asked the first.

"They think that the baby they have taken care of is the only one that is precious!"

"I don't believe that," said the first angel. "I believe we really have taken care of the most beautiful one! Oh! Take a look at what is happening right now in our little treasure."

With her now healthy rose-color and lovingly beating heart, the newborn baby developed an unexpected behavior. She wouldn't close her eyes. It wasn't that she couldn't. She actually didn't want to. But that meant that the baby wouldn't sleep. Mommy didn't know what was going on. She tried everything she could think of to soothe her baby to sleep, but nothing seemed to help. Her baby would not close her eyes. Very soon, Baby and Mommy were exhausted, and this new situation went on endlessly.

The two angels, observing what was taking place, were glad they had decided to stick around.

They began thinking. Finally, the first angel spoke, "What could be wrong? Heart is beautifully beating, body is pink, but eyes are open. Did we make a mistake?"

"Oh come on," said the second angel. "Stop thinking as humans do, looking for what we did wrong. You know that as angels, we do not believe in making mistakes. If the baby's eyes are open, taking endless delight with the fact of its life, that is just the way it has to be, this is how this baby's story goes. She's excited to be rescued."

The first angel interrupted, "I am sure you are right, but rescued or not, she is still a baby and needs to sleep. She can't wait for reasons to justify her being different in that respect, just take a look! Mommy and Baby are both exhausted! We are going to have to intervene once again."

"Well," said the second angel, "we are here to join her in her story, so let's find out what we think we can do."

Both angels began thinking. "Baby will not close her eyes…hmmm… what would that be?" The first angel closed his eyes in order to find out what that meant. It felt like a way to avoid something. "Oh naughty one," said the second angel watching the first, "are you the one now closing your eyes? For what reason do you do that?"

The first quickly answered, "I wanted to see what the baby would experience if she did close her eyes. I wanted to see what the baby was trying to keep from happening by leaving her eyes open."

"And what was that?" asked the second angel.

"At first I thought she was afraid to stop seeing the beauty of life," answered the angel. "But now, with my own eyes closed, I can see what she would see if she allowed herself to close hers. You know what I see? I see Black."

"Black?" repeated the second angel.

"Yes, and that is the answer, I see Black…Black! That's it! When humans close their eyes, everything goes black!!!"

"And are you excited about that?" asked the second angel. "It sounds to me like that's simply sad, to lose all colors…or am I not understanding something?"

The first angel patiently explained. "Remember we asked Black to come help us so that our work could be done? Heavenly work on earth has to be done in the dark. We had to bring Black in order to get enough darkness to properly reassemble the little heart. So that's it!" exclaimed the angel. "Now that it's fully alive, the baby doesn't want Black! I mean, her pink little heart does not want to go back to black, for it was during Black's stay that this heart was taken away from the body. Can't you see that the little pink heart is driving the baby to avoid Black so that it won't be separated again from the rest of the baby's body?"

This made sense to the second angel, who remained silent.

Wondering how to intervene in the situation that both of them now understood, the two angels kept closely observing what was starting to happen on it's own, with little baby's inability to close her eyes and go to sleep. At the same time, the mother was also observing her baby girl. Exhausted as she was, she could still tenderly speak to her daughter. Looking into the open eyes of her beautiful but very tired baby, she said, "Sweetheart, I wish you could tell me what is going on. Why wouldn't you sleep? How can I help you?"

The baby did not answer immediately in any way, but one day, on a very clear day, the kind of day that makes all colors bright under a blue and sunny sky, the sheets and diapers gleamed white on the clothesline with freshness that only a warm sun can imbue. The baby, looking over at the brilliant white sheets and then down at the fresh white diapers the mother had placed on her body, was able to close her eyes and take a short nap. Observing how the brightness of the day had allowed her daughter to sleep as if at peace, the mommy remembered that soon after her daughter was born, there had been a sudden eclipse, a black episode in which nobody could see anything. For the first time, the mother realized that this must have been so very hard on her new baby. Maybe that was why her daughter felt such a continuous need for light! This girl needed more brightness, more brilliance around her than most people! With that in mind, a strange new idea occurred to the mother. Even though it was her own and strongly doubted it, the idea wouldn't leave her mind. The idea that would not stop teasing the baby's mother was this: "My baby girl needs White!" So the mother began fantasizing how she could make sure that White would fill up her daughter's life, whitening mind and body for long periods of time without interruption. "Would that really help her sleep?" she wondered…but the thought only buzzed louder. "Your baby needs White, and needs it all the time." So without having answers as to why this would possibly work, the mother decided to give White a try. She had to see if it would help her daughter sleep the same way she had on that bright sunny day when white had been the color that was most brilliant of all, making it seem like the soul of light itself.

At first she thought, maybe I can give her more milk. But the baby couldn't see the whiteness of the milk when she was nursing. So how would the baby even realize that milk was white? To recreate the unconscious bliss of nursing, she was not willing to bottle feed this baby, who would only close her eyes when sucking on the nipple of the bottle anyway. Finally, after a lot of thinking, the mother came up with the idea of offering her baby something that she would surely want to look at as well as chew and swallow—something the baby could participate in while incorporating White. The mother knew just what this could be: small, round pieces of homeopathic candy with healing potential became clear on account of their luminous white color. Where her baby was concerned, the mother hoped that the sweetness of the candy and its bright white color could be associated in the baby's mind, and be a way of leading her to incorporate White that was entirely missing during that strange dark period of black near the beginning of her life. In order to make the small round white candies taste even sweeter, the mother soaked them in a special loving liquid she had prepared, something her own mother had used to sweeten things for her when she was small. No one knows just how it is made, but this old tradition of the sweetened candies certainly worked for the baby. She loved to taste them and decided to play a candy game. To make discovering their whiteness fun, she would hide them in the baby's favorite stuffed bear's beard. The baby, by now, was already crawling, would find the precious pieces of small round white candy, and having fun finding them. The baby liked this game and would immediately take each candy she discovered into her mouth, just as her mother had hoped. Mother of course did not really know what she was actually doing, other than following an instinctive idea. She was offering the one thing she felt sure could cure her daughter's long lack of rest.

Every single day, week after week, month after month, the mother played the candy game. Always guided by one clear thought—she loved her baby and had been blessed to have her. The two angels who had been closely observing the situation with utmost care were clapping their wings in joy. "This is so great!" they said to each other. "If Mommy only knew the transcendence of what she is doing!!!" What they observed, was that the cobblestone candies soaked in love and care that the mother was giving in loving play to her baby were nothing other than a bridge being built. They were in awe of human ingenuity. "We had been wondering how to help, and just take a look, who would have imagined how in naive play, Mother and Baby would find a way to put together this beautiful bridge!" "It is marvelous!" said the second angel. "It takes away all reason for the heart to fear being apart from the body. The fear was created by the blackness that kept Mother and Baby and Heart and Body from seeing that they can always be connected. The luminous bridge has taken away this fear. Even better, it makes separation an adventure, something to be traversed, not feared. Black and White, Mother and Baby, Heart and Body, all now capable of connecting with each other. Isn't the arrival of the bridge a wonderful thing? And isn't it great that they played it into being?"

While this talk between the angels went on, the mother found another reason to be pleased. Her baby girl could now close her eyes and receive the divine renewal that only sleep can bring, even though she was still not so fond of darkness and would rather be playing than sleeping. Nevertheless, when she has to, she can rest. She can trust herself to fall asleep, because she intuitively knows the white bridge will be there to bring into her the happy world of wakefulness again. Even more important, her body can rest, secure in having a pink beautiful heart that is confidently sharing the flow of life. And as only the angels can verify, her soul can rest too, trusting that when the baby wakes up, there will be light once again, and there will be mommy around to welcome her to the new day. Within herself, of course, the baby will never stop playing, and so she will find her own bridge again and again. As she grows older, she will gradually discover the courage she has in her healthy pink heart. This heart is really the hero of her story, for it was brave enough to weather all the difficulties. If the courageous heart had not chosen to stay alive, neither the watchful angels nor her creative ingenious mother could have done the good they did for this beautiful baby to remain alive and go on creating her very own life story.

A LITTLE PIECE OF ME

There was once a land in which monsters liked to arrive. For some unknown reason, they always wanted to participate in anything that looked like a happy life. It was understood in the land, that into the homes and meeting places of people of all ages, one or even more than one monster suddenly would appear. There was also no doubt that it was mainly children who had the honesty to accept that they had seen these monsters and so it was they who reported on what they saw. Older people who didn't like to question the security of their happy life would wonder why the children allowed themselves to see monsters at all. The truth was, everyone was scared that they appeared in the midst of the happiness that ruled that land. Little did the adults know, that in their lack of recognition of the monsters that kept appearing, they were themselves beginning to act like monsters. This is always what happens when fear is growing within a population and only children are willing to express it openly. This silent fear constitutes the most important nutrient for the monsters empowerment and is exactly the food from which they get fed. Monsters are always enriched and enlivened by fear that cannot be expressed.

Accordingly, when the monsters arrived, they would quickly appear to the children, but in any crowd, they kept themselves mostly invisible to the adults, or the grown-ups would totally deny them. That way, when a trembling child would scream and try to say he or she had seen or heard a monster, the impotent adults would most likely turn to the child, and with a harsh voice set to a scolding tone:

"What is the matter with you? Stop crying, nothing is going on for you to cry like this!" And of course that attempt to silence fear only made everyone much more scared. After all, they could still hear the child sobbing and begging, "Please listen, I am not making this up. There are monsters here!" But each child who tried to articulate the dreadful apparition he or she had seen got a totally unsympathetic retort from the nearest adult, "I will not listen to you if you do not stop crying, this is not the way to talk, if you want something, say it, and say it in a nice way! But stop pretending you have seen a monster."

In the loneliness of their feeling left in the same fearful state, children would try again to get some adult to believe them. "But I am telling the truth, please…!" And each child would get an even more monstrous answer, "It seems that today, you shouldn't be among people at all, you need to be alone, when you are ready to behave, then you may come out."

In this way, the monsters were taking more and more of the life of the community into themselves. Now, not only did the monsters manage to scare the little ones, they also evoked other monsters in the vicinity of the very adults who felt too proud to deal with what they saw and felt as "childish issues." A war seemed to go on between the arriving monsters and the evoked monsters. A few adults even recognized some of the monsters, but most of them were simply denied by the adult population. In this way, not only were the children affected by the existence of these monsters, but also by the unexpressed fears of the adults around them. The whole population was becoming more and more frightened of the monstrous life in their midst.

The situation got so out of hand in the land, that the wisest of the old women and men who had been around long enough to remember what it was like to live in this land without fear, realized they had to do something. These wise old ones suggested a gathering to discuss relevant issues that were consuming the peace, as the monsters have done in the past. After a long and arduous discussion, they came to the conclusion that it was essential to begin a dialogue with the monsters themselves. To get such a dialogue started, the wise elders counseled that the very next time someone in the community was threatened by a monster causing mounting panic, that person, for the first time in this land's history, invite the monster to come to the gathering place for a talk. It was planned that this whole talk take place during a special gathering in which only the wisest old men and women would be allowed to attend. Only in this special setting would any monster have a chance to talk, and be really heard by any human the monster had frightened.

The group of greatly respected elders gave notice to all the inhabitants of this monster-preferred land, as to the agreement that had been made. When it was heard by the citizens, a man who had been severely attacked and repeatedly scared by one of the monsters, stood up and said, "Whoever has to do that will not survive!" He explained his outburst by addressing the elders directly, "Do you mean to say that you are opening the door for any number of these monsters to come into our homes and be our guests?" No one had ever questioned the elders like this before, but he went on. "You would suggest this when they are threatening our lives?" And then he said something that was absolutely unprecedented. "Why didn't you invite the people to participate when you discussed such an important issue that affects their lives?" One of the elders, replied, "You heard us right, and you need to know that we will be here to support whomever is attacked next. We will defend you as needed and as we have always done, we will protect you forever. You have to realize that we are the old ones who have already lived a full life, and we are ready to risk ourselves. If something should happen as a result of you following our daring proposition, we will be there—not the people and not your children or anybody else within our land. It is our sacred duty to protect you and take care of the situation that develops. Then we will find out if our taking care of you only result in creating more fleeing refugees and developing more hiding places in order to keep you safe, or whether we have found a much more radical way to enable you to go on leading peaceful, happy lives within the safety of your own homes.

This statement seemed to calm people down. Now, when hearing the news of what had been decided, people stopped questioning it, and began talking about who would be willing to cooperate with such a difficult and challenging task as letting the monsters in, since no one really wanted to do it. One immediate result was that no one definitively declared even seeing a monster. That was one way to postpone the fear of the monsters' eventual appearance in their homes. On the other hand, it was clearly established in principle that whomever would be attacked next would invite the deeply rejected monster to stay and talk in the gathering with the wise old men and women.

Following a consensus of this radical agreement, it did not take long before a rather frail woman, who looked as vulnerable as if she were an unprotected girl, to admit she was once again being attacked by the monsters. As it had happened many times before, she cried out, "I am scared! I don't want this! I want to vomit, I am afraid, I'm going to die, I don't have the strength to go on like this!" This gave the elders an opportunity to show their empathic response to a citizen who was frightened. One of them said directly to the scared woman, "You are not going to die, it is going to be fine, the monsters will soon stop attacking, we are with you and everything will be just as it has always been before. Trust us, please do what we say."

This frail woman-child was told that she was the first one selected to invite a monster into her home. She would be accompanied by a group of elders, and they would help her talk with the monsters. Naturally, between bouts of crying and sobbing, the woman-child said, "I can't do this, I don't want to do it. Monsters bite every piece of happiness, they hurt, and they swallow people's joy and everything else that makes someone willing to live!" The elders who heard her felt deep concern for this woman's childish fear.

Nevertheless, they reiterated their conviction that she had to extend an invitation to the monster that had most recently threated her. To take care of her feelings, they said, "We know how scary this is, but we will be with you at all times, we will join and protect you, you are not alone, in fact, we think that you…" With tears, the woman-child interrupted, "There is one little piece of me left, a hidden piece that has not been hurt, a very little piece of who I used to be that can still enjoy living. It can't be seen nor touched by anyone. It's all I have left. You want me to risk that little piece to the mercy of monsters. But monsters take all! They intrude to profane all of anyone. If I invite them in, I won't be able to stop them from swallowing the little piece left of me. I can't risk it! That little piece of me allows me to exist simply by being apart from everything that threatens me. I have survived so far entirely as a consequence of it. Therefore, it must remain hidden. If you have your wisdom, you will understand this. Please don't make me do this dangerous thing."

Hearing this frail woman-child speaking her deepest truth, the elders found themselves in tears at the suffering they were witnessing. But even though many elders were deeply touched to the point of silently reconsidering the recommendation that they had made in light of the woman's continued expression of fear, it was too late to do anything.

For before the elders could express a change of heart, a harsh, deep and distant voice was already making itself heard:

"Here I am."

The woman began trembling as she heard this voice; one she knew all too well belonged to one of the worst monsters. And this time, she knew that she couldn't run away, because that was the way to be eternally chased. She realized that what the elders had been telling her was right. What she had to do now was to remain in the presence of the monster, with the elders to help her find her own voice. She seemed to hear them speaking in soft voices to say, "We are with you, you are not alone, we won't leave you." As she felt the support of the kind elders' voices, she was able to summon the courage to finally utter words she had wanted to say for a very long time.

"Get out of my life!!!! Leave me alone! Stop scaring me! Just go away!" but as she said that, the harsh voice answered in its deep, unmistakable tone.

"I don't believe you really want to be alone, and that you don't want me to scare you."

Not expecting that answer, the woman-child grew pale. She couldn't refrain from asking, "Who are you?"

"I am a guardian of treasures, I protect secrets that have been forgotten. My only way to do so is to make you be afraid of me."

Having heard this response, which from a monster did not sound at all threatening, the woman wanted to ask other questions, "Are all monsters guardians? I never saw you as guardians; you were so ugly and so horrible! You didn't talk, you attacked!"

"Ugly? Horrible? Were we? We can't see or hear ourselves, you know, but talking to you today, it kind of feels nice to be seen and heard. Why do you call us ugly and horrible?" The woman was astounded that one monster's voice had become a multitude.

Everybody else present was incredulous too at being able to hear the conversation that had emerged. They were amazed at the force with which the woman replied.

"You are horrible because you are huge! You are horrible because you are intrusive. You are horrible because you scare children and people like me who have remained children. If you could hear your own voices, you would feel as threatened as I am. Why do I have to tell you that your voices are frightening?" The answer the woman received was actually quite touching.

"We have been for a very long time silently keeping secrets, without being able to talk. Our voices carry the rasp of this very long silence."

The dialogue seemed to have been established between the woman and the monsters, and with such wondrous thoroughness that no other voice was now heard.

"Why haven't you talked before?" The woman asked the monster, in a totally naïve tone.

"Because nobody wants to listen to us, even though we try…" The monster stopped midsentence, apparently in an effort to be fair. And very slowly, the monster said, "Only at very specific times do we get to be heard. They happen, but so seldom that we forget fast."

This answer seemed to empower the woman. "May I ask," she said, "what then are the treasures that you have kept to yourselves for so very many years?"

She got a quick, but evasive answer, "They are to be discovered by each one."

She went on, "You sound as if you are talking about surprises, but do you really feel anyone would welcome a surprise coming from a monster? Of course not."

"It couldn't be wanted because it is unknown, and anyway you people wouldn't know what to do with the surprising things we might tell you."

"These surprising treasures that you take care of and have kept to yourselves, don't they have any instructions?"

"No, they don't carry instructions on their backs, and neither do we. We ourselves have forgotten what to do with our surprises since we have kept quiet for so very long."

Forgotten? Am I not understanding?" said the woman. "Are you saying that nobody knows what to do with the treasures at your disposal, not even you?"

"Look, you have to find out for yourself what to do with anything that comes from us. That is your individual task, and I am afraid you can only accomplish it by taking what we can give you and try livening with them."

That didn't satisfy the woman's curiosity and she went on asking. "How do you even know they are treasures?"

"Well, I guess that's what anything that can enrich people's lives is called."

To which the woman countered, "I thought treasures were beautiful things—things that you like, that you want, that makes you happy, good things that have value for oneself."

"The treasures that we take care of are neither good nor bad for people in the long run. They are a mystery, they are actually an adventure to be discovered, and the adventure makes the life of the discoverer richer."

"Well, if that's how you look at it, a risky adventure at my expense, I certainly prefer you not coming to me with any treasures. I have to tell you, you still scare me to death, and I see no enrichment in my life when you give me more than I already have to be afraid of."

"You must know there is more than one kind of treasure."

"I'm sure. But how blind and insensitive can I be that I don't see any value in any of them?"

"Did you hear how scared you sound?"

"No, I don't have to hear it, it is enough with what I feel."

"Can you also feel then, the strength of your fear? Can you feel the power of its grip on you? You see yourself as the frail, tiny, and weak woman, but you certainly feel very strong! I think what I have been keeping intact is the knowledge of how strong you really are. I am fearsome to you because you have not dared to know how strong you are. The farther you live away from the strength of your being, the more afraid you are going to feel and the more monstrous I am going to seem to you. We both agree; you have one life to live, why would you hate me so much for wanting you to shine with your own light and enlighten this world with what only you can bring? When I say that, though, you somehow darken my message and hear it in a monstrous way."

The woman, now petrified, said in an appalled, small voice, "I only have a very little piece of me left...and..."

Everyone hoped she would continue her brave dialogue with the monster, but now there was only silence. No voice was heard. Neither hers, nor the monster's. In fact, the woman was in tears, and the monster was gone. All conversation had ended.

Time passed, of course, but no one dared to ask what would come next after such an experience. Soul matters, as you know, are intimate, always keeping their mystery.

The only one thing known by everyone privileged to listen to this rare exchange between the terrified woman and her monster was that the frail sensitive woman had dared to converse with the monster. Oh, and one other thing: she did not only survive to become a part of the community, but in later years, she was willing to say that conversing with one's own monster was something to recommend, and perhaps should be attempted by any member of the community who had ever felt attacked by a monster.

The truth was, the once-frail sensitive woman-child had now become a wise old woman. She became a member of the group of wise women, not because of her age, but because she had demonstrated that she was able to relate to her very own monster, which took hard, soulful work.

She had done so with "the little piece of herself." And she found out that monsters do not disappear just because they are confronted directly, but rather become part of a life story. In this way, she discovered that we belong to a much larger world, one that is beyond our reason to understand, and our heart to embrace, where the ultimate purpose of life is just to maintain the dialogue, or is it a dance, with all the parts of ourselves, including those parts that frighten us most.

As for the land, that place where monsters used to arrive as if summoned solely by their own energy, that land became known as the place where monsters not only appeared to scare people, but when they did, they talk with its inhabitants. Like all lands, this land knew the seasons of the year—warm and beautiful, as well as gray, cold and icy at times. It enjoyed watching overhead the movement of the moon and the stars. It shivered through black scary nights and thrilled to the silvery illuminations that would come and go through them. In this land, people had actually learned something. They had finally found out that by living much closer to the monsters who had always scared them, they had not only begun to be less scared, but also to act less monstrously themselves. Now, the greatest adventure they knew was seeing and hearing themselves, and that became, to everyone's surprise, the most cherishable of all life's treasures.

THE STORY OF AN EAR

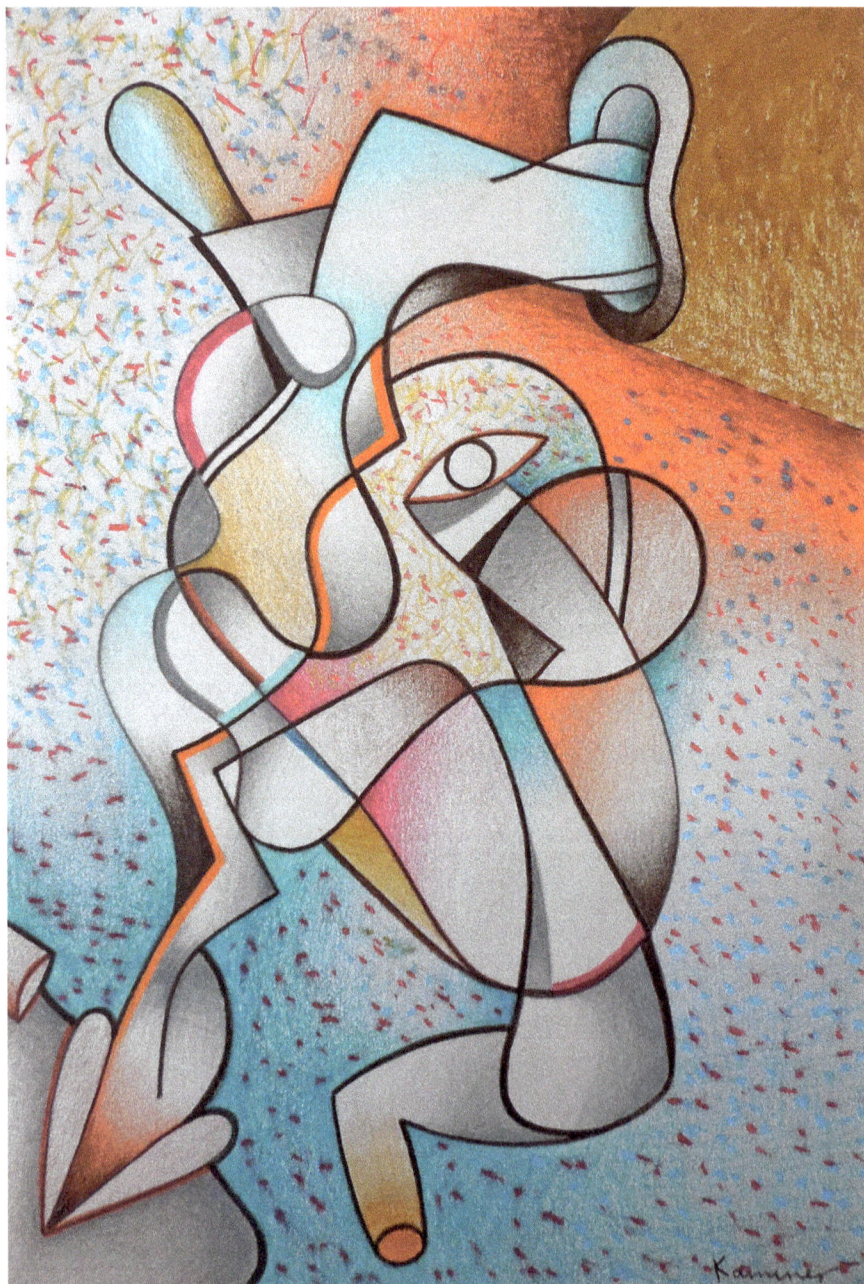

Once upon a time, there was an Ear, an Ear that became so important in the Body kingdom that he became the subject and main character of this story. It all started one day when Ear got plugged. For many years, Ear had been faithfully fulfilling his duty in the Body kingdom without occurring to him to do anything else. In inquiring of himself what could possibly be happening, he was surprised to discover that he desperately wanted to be heard. Somewhere in his bones, he realized the cessation of movement had forced him to attend to them in a new way, that their present stillness was actually holding a feeling. All of his life, ever since he was created, the unfair one-sidedness of being forced to hear everything everybody else had to say just felt oppressive. Tired of his duty, Ear was now at a point where he wanted and actually needed to be heard. Plugged as he had become from so much hearing, filled with a seemingly overwhelming flooding, he found himself painfully begging for someone else to hear him out.

Nose smelled this pain and was also affected by Ear's total congestion, and soon, the pain was affecting the whole of the Body kingdom. So let me tell you a little bit about the Body kingdom. This was a rich and beautiful kingdom, amazingly well designed, with plenty of resources. It actually had been the inspiration for artists, scientists, and even psychologists for years and years. Everyone in the kingdom had always worked hard to serve the entire community with respect, and to live up to the particular task each one had, but despite all this effort, the day had finally come that Ear's pain appeared. This new complication spoke to another important character that now became part of our story—her name was Voice. Voice, who had long sensed that something was out of order in the kingdom, and rarely, held back when the time had come to talk, said, "Excuse me, someone else wanting to say something? That's nonsense of course because who could be talking other than me, if I am the only one who does the talking! I hope I am not talking to myself."

But at this time, someone else was indeed, with tremendous effort, saying something—it was Ear! He managed to mumble, "I want to be heard, could you please help me, Voice?"

Voice really had to rouse herself now. Shaking herself, which meant turning and jumping around all the pitches she had at her command in the melodic scale, and to her great annoyance beginning to be out of tune, and even losing her proper rhythm, she spoke again, "I don't know what is going on here, but it is making me feel very uncomfortable. I, who is nothing but Voice, am even beginning to believe, I can hear! But how could I be hearing something? I don't hear, and it cannot be someone else because I am the one who has to do the talking. I hope you know that talking takes energy. Even the time it takes is an effort to arrange. Nevertheless, talking is my job. In my position, I cannot afford to stop talking. After all, I was created to talk! And I do my job. Not that I get paid or anything like that, but what else can a voice do other than talk?"

Hearing this proud speech, Ear felt even more pressure than before. And remember, it was already plugged with infectious water. So despite his delight at hearing Voice raise herself to her very highest level, he could tell that his hearing had begun to suffer. Now that he was in such pain, oh, how he longed for someone who could hear him. Thinking he was only speaking to himself, Ear said, "It must be great to be heard."

And Voice, even though her entire life up to now had mostly been consumed in endless talking just to justify her existence, must have heard him, because she answered back. "Well, to tell you the truth, I am not so sure that when I speak I am always heard, because to be honest, I can't hear a thing, I can only talk, but, wait…isn't there someone out there talking?"

"Am I not able to hear? And am I not answering back? I have never had an interchange before, for of course I was not made to hear, but to tell everyone the truth, I have often felt quite lonely. So now I have to pinch myself—is there really now someone else talking? Because if so… then maybe, I could finally rest a bit! I can even imagine that if I could take such a rest, I could even get to hear something…" Now talking to herself, "You know, I never thought about it…oh dear, with all the talking one cannot even think!"

Then, something even more incredible happened. In the midst of this dialogue, limited as it was by the rigid and regular roles Ear and Voice had always had to play in the kingdom, a sparkle of mischievous light appeared in the space where Voice and Ear were having their conversation. Riding on that sparkle as if it were a magical vehicle, Ear let himself be delivered right to the very doorstep of Voice. Kneeling before her, he said, "Would you let me borrow your speaking instrument? I don't know how to use it because I have never had one, but maybe if I try…perhaps I could use it to help me heal my pain?"

Not surprisingly, such a bold proposition was received by Voice initially with proud contempt. She immediately responded, "Why? What a silly thing to say! If I lend you my voice, with what am I going to say anything? After all, I have nothing else! I am only Voice! What am I going to do in life if I stop my talking and let others in the kingdom, who have no experience at all in using my instrument, start doing the talking? I will be out of business. I might even die! And what would happen to the kingdom? Just hearing you propose something like this, using what sounds to me like a voice, I am already afraid of dying!

Then Ear, hearing the distress that he had apparently caused, very softly answered, "But I will lend you my hearing."

And then their engagement began in earnest; I should really call it a dance. Of course, our characters, Voice and Ear, were not quite aware of the particular choreography they were interpreting, which was composed of constant shifting movements that brought them together with *pirouettes*, *grand jeté*, and gracious *pas de deux*, but I can tell you it was fascinating! It was also a bit disconcerting from the standpoint of the usual harmony of the kingdom, since their movements, though authentic and true to the unusual circumstance that had brought them to take this brave steps to try to "speak" to each other, were so new that they had really not been seen in the kingdom ever before! But doesn't such dancing take place in most of the fairy tales? I can only tell you, I can still see the princess Voice and the prince Ear dancing together, as if they had done so always, in the Body's castle. But as to how the other inhabitants of that conservative realm felt about their doing so, is even now too soon to tell. At the time, of course, no one else was saying anything, and Voice and Ear didn't care, because for them, with all the confusion that was taking place in the Kingdom of Body, the only important thing, as they knew, was to go on dancing. In truth, their dancing with each other was just as new to them as to everyone else, but only they knew that the life of the kingdom depended on it.

And so choreography began, Ear and Voice danced out their gifts to each other in an ever more loving interchange. I can still experience it now. Ear is talking, and Voice is hearing. Their kingdom is being shown the value of their newly acquired gifts, coming from the loving trade they made, and now can draw upon to exchange and give back, over and over again, as they move together and apart in the Kingdom of Body's first-ever dance.

While being on display in this way, the partners had many other experiences too. For their dance was their first step out into a world that extended even beyond their own kingdom. I cannot tell you all the adventures they had in that larger place, the World, but I can relate that a time arrived when Ear and Voice wanted to summarize their adventures with each other, in and outside the kingdom. Ear, now having a voice, and being the one who in the very first place created the chaos in the kingdom, is the one who now began this final talking:

"I must confess something. I do so not to avoid responsibility for my deeds. You know, Voice, I did not plan this adventure, and I didn't get to choose the chaos that began it either. What I couldn't say until you lent me your instrument, though, is that, I believe both the chaos and the adventures came from another source. We both know we are living in a fairy tale. And many times I have heard that in every fairy tale there is magic. Well, in our story, there were those sparkles that I *heard* and rode. They gave us the idea that we too could dance…I heard them before I realized anything was wrong with me. It must have been the sound of rain that went on to moisten the kingdom, or perhaps just the beat of a fairy stick that touched the kingdom because you know, the same day I heard those uncanny sounds, I happened to be playing around with Eye, and he told me that he had seen some sparkles shining, just then. I cannot remember exactly the sequence of events that happened next, but very soon after, came my first realization that I was plugged. I do remember thinking, what is going on? And what should I do? For the very first time in my life, I was in pain. I needed help, but who am I, but Ear, to ask for help? And that was when I realized I didn't have a voice. I could not express what I was feeling—I had no way at all to talk. No one was able to hear me—only me—because I was an ear and an ear only! So I found myself trying and trying to communicate, beyond my means, and once again, there was magic, because suddenly you were able to hear me! The sparkles returned at that point, and we started playing, and suddenly, I proposed—proposed that you lend me your voice, and I my hearing, and with that we became the sparkles, we became the magic of the kingdom. We began the choreography of authentic engagement and took that out into the world…"

"The last thing I need to tell you, Voice, is what it was like for me, Ear, being in the world, having borrowed your amazing instrument. I don't think I have to say that having a voice in the world isn't only a blessing. Do I have to tell you that I felt scared to death? I was so unexperienced! How does one use a voice? I thought. Not having an answer from you, I had to find out for myself. So I hesitantly began slowly talking, and as I practiced, it actually began to feel okay—this talking, and finally it even felt good! So I went on talking and talking and talking even more until I got so big with talking the plug just fell out!"

"The next morning when I woke up, pretty much restored to myself, except for the extra gift you had lent me, for the first time in my life I thought, what good can talking be if one is not heard? You see, my friend Voice, while using your amazing instrument, I came to realize that for any voice to have meaning, it also needs to be heard, and not just heard by the other one who is being spoken to, but also by oneself. And that brought me back to what an ear is for, to enable someone to listen to himself. After that discovery, I knew I could give you your instrument back, for I knew I had what I needed already!"

"But of course, as you know, I didn't give you your instrument back right away. I was enjoying having a voice, even though it was only on loan. I needed it just a little bit longer to appreciate fully my own capacity for hearing."

"So I went on exploring what is the hearing really about. It was then when I discovered that hearing is a way of receiving something other in oneself. And I also found out that hearing fully, takes more than the ears, it needs a capacity to recognize what is essential. In our kingdom, that is called Heart. It needs a way to be open to the world and differentiate what is experienced there—our kingdom calls that Mind. It needs something with which to trust the unfolding of the future, and that our kingdom calls Intuition. And of course it needs channels and walls to perceive and close off the world we get such an earful of—our kingdom calls those Senses. And true hearing needs what the kingdom calls Compassion, to make room for all the different ways of suffering that all these parts of the Body kingdom can get themselves into. My plug was only one. Luckily I discovered that all these capacities for function, for suffering and for enjoying are the very life of the Kingdom of Body, and knowing that taught me the greatest lesson of all, that I need never imagine I am alone doing all the work of bringing order to our kingdom's cacophony because the job is bigger than any Ear could ever manage to do alone. So now I want to thank you, for while I was discovering all the things I did while I listened to the voice you lent me, I also heard the first murmurings of a voice that was growing in me. This was not the instrument you lent me. It was a different one, with a different sound, all of my own. I was able to tease its sound out from the sound of your voice, because, as I hope you will remember, I am a specialist in hearing. It's what I do. Trust me, this was a new voice, not your voice. Yes, as strange as it may sound, an ear can have a voice, and I do believe this one that I was finally hearing was my own…!"

Then his friend Voice that had been very patiently listening, interrupted and said, "Well, now that I have hearing, let me tell you what I discovered while we were sharing the same adventures: Being able to move out in an authentic way from my very little world, after I had the courage to accept your daring proposition, I discovered something that has humbled me, and I was the proudest figure in the Kingdom of Body. I discovered that we all have a voice! Not that we all use it. I had that distinction, thank heaven, and certainly, nor the very same type of voice as I have trained all these years, but—well let's just say that there are other ways to communicate besides being a soprano, you know…? This is hard even for me to put into words, so let me start from the very beginning: When I first got quiet because of lending you my voice, I was in terror. I thought I had lost my instrument forever. I had become a very long silence, more than what I thought I was capable to endure. I felt indeed that I was a living death, for only death could be that silent, and only someone still living could know how terrible that silence was, and then, in that terrible silence I suddenly discovered that I could hear something being said. What I heard was not exactly a voice as I have known myself to be, it was something else, an audible gesture—a gesture expressing compassion, and not just that, there were the eyes, there was light shining in them, and a face smiling, and then there was this posture that I couldn't quite understand because I have never spoken that language, and arms and legs. Am I making myself clear? Somewhere in me, not just around me, *in* me, the whole Body kingdom was moving, each part of it joining in with its own instrument, and through a voice that was speaking for the *whole* of that, it was actually communicating! It was so alive. I could hear the breathing, and feel the rhythm, the shine and moisture on the skin! After hearing this speech of the *whole* for a wonderful while, I even began understanding that every part of the kingdom had its own language. Yes, I discovered that all sorts of possibilities for voice, for communication, for making oneself heard, were there, as long as I, despite my own instrument, kept silent. That *was* a discovery!! I suddenly felt as if I had wings, and I could fly, because when I realized that everything in our kingdom has a voice, I knew for the first time in my loud life that my job and even myself are not as important as I had imagined we were. Oh, I can tell you, my life became lighter! And brighter! I then knew, that even if you never gave my instrument back, I could still talk and also, be silent and rest, and while resting, I could hear the soundless voices that I never knew before, not a bit less important than my own talking, which I still love doing."

That being said and heard, Voice gave Ear his instrument back, and of course he reciprocated. And from that day on, Voice and Ear, who by now knew they would always be dearest friends, found it easiest simply to go on dancing in the Kingdom of Body. Grateful to one another, they made friends, played together and enjoyed the games that occurred to them. Their very favorite games to play were, "hide and seek" and "let's pretend." And so they used to say, "Let's hide and look after one another, and let's pretend that we disappear, and then let's find each other and discover ourselves each time as new, but whatever games we play, let's be friends, and go on playing again and again."

And in this magic way, Ear and Voice played together happily ever after, in the most authentic of movements.

I am most greatful to the IAAP for permission to include this story, which was first published in: Kiehl, Emilija, Editor, Copenhagen 2013: *100 years on: Origins, Innovation and Controversies, Proceedings of the 18th Congress of the International Association for Analytical Psychology,* 2014, Daimon, Einsideln.

THE CROWN

Once upon a time, in a recently found land, a huge and beautiful kingdom was built. A fair and smart king and an embracing wise queen governed the prosperous kingdom with its hardworking inhabitants. This was a land where people not only felt grateful to belong, but also proud of forming such community. Even though joy was what mostly characterized the kingdom, including the king and the queen, among all the blessings they were able to recognize, there was nevertheless one fact that kept them sad and deeply longing—the king and the queen were unable to have a child.

Without missing to fulfill their duties with their people, both King and Queen would everyday pray to be blessed with the good fortune of having a child. They prayed to the gods, their ancestors and all the generations that have reigned the kingdom before them to help them conceive a child. It was one day, at dusk, when the sun was fading and the new moon had barely began to appear in the sky, and a star, the first one to appear, was particularly shiny, that the queen noticed its special glow in a way that she had never seen before. It was nine months after that night that the greatly expected child arrived. The parents' prayers had been heard and a baby son was born.

The new parents hosted a magnificent party to celebrate the arrival of their son. They invited everyone in the kingdom that wanted to assist. Music, lights, dance, delicious food, and hundreds of guests arrived to welcome the much-expected baby. During the party, the king and the queen not only announced the birth of their very first son, but also pronounced the future king to their people and for the first time placed over his very little head the crown he would be wearing when he becomes King. Overwhelmed with joy, the king and the queen forgot to take off the crown from the baby's little head. The crown was left on until the parents finally remembered to remove it from the baby's head. By then, the crown had already left a mark on the baby's forehead. The marking seemed to be really painful because of the baby's endless crying.

Faced with the circumstances, the queen worried for her child's well-being and the painful scar that wouldn't vanish from the baby's forehead. Not wanting to lose time, that same night, she asked the medicine man to come see the scar that was provoking her baby's endless crying. The medicine man did not attend the party. He was sitting at home waiting since he intuitively felt that an emergency was going to take place and that he would be called in. He just didn't know where he would need to go. It turned out to be that he was called to the very same palace where the newly arrived baby was pronounced to be eventual King.

As soon as the medicine man arrived at the palace, he carefully examined the crying baby. He found that it was indeed a healthy child, but as he saw the baby's painful mark on his forehead he said, "With all due respect my Lady, I believe that the crown was rudely imposed over the baby's head far too soon. It must be heavy and the baby's head is yet too tender to be able to hold a crown." He then kept quiet. As the queen heard him, she anxiously asked, "But when will he heal?" "That is an answer I can't give you my Lady. He seems to be a strong and healthy baby, but I don't really know how the mark on the baby's head will evolve, it is too soon to tell since…" The queen anxiously interrupted, "But will the mark heal? What are we to do?" The medicine man answered as honest as he possibly could, "He seems to be a particularly sensitive baby. For now I can only suggest to put some ice over his scar, which should help with the pain." Then, in a meditative mode, he added, "We will have to wait and pay close attention to see how the child develops. I am sure you will take good care of him. Please let me know any time if I can be of any further help."

The medicine man left. The king who was so excited about his new son went on celebrating. Meanwhile, the queen was feeling heartbroken because of her baby's endless crying. Having carefully heard what the medicine man had mentioned, she decided that paying close attention to her son's wellbeing was to become her main priority. Submerged in the uncertainty of what could come to her son, she instructed everyone involved in her child's upbringing to let her know if they noticed any change in the prince's health. The teachers that were to be in charge of his son's education were advised as well. The king tried to comfort his highly distressed wife by saying he would support her decisions regarding their son's wellbeing and participate in whatever is necessary. The king was convinced that God had blessed them with this beautiful baby and that nothing should interfere with him becoming the future king, as had been the family tradition for generations and generations.

Time went by and the baby grew up. He became a beautiful child who carried a mark on his forehead, imprinted the day he was introduced as the future king—a mark that was there to remain forever. In the same way as healthy children do, the boy liked playing, running around, jumping and hiding. He also attended classes especially designed for what his future tasks, as a king would require. Teachers from different parts of the world were hired to teach the child their own native language, culture, history, art and mythology. It was important for the future king to learn about the rest of the world, as well as his own land.

One of the foreign teachers was a rather small, fat, and dark-skinned woman. Her name was Mercedes Marin, whose specialty was the Nahuatl mythology. She was so passionate about her culture that it was not difficult for almost anyone who heard her talk to be caught in the magnificent stories that she narrated. The future king was no exception. He deeply enjoyed hearing how the world was created according to the Nahuatl mythology, the relationships among the gods, how men were brought into existence, all framed by the love she felt for her culture.

Among the myths that this teacher taught the future king, there was one that particularly drew the child's attention—the myth of Quetzalcoatl. This important character was a prince, a priest, and a God according to the Nahuatl and the Mayan mythology. He found himself involved in a situation in which he did not behave according to what he believed in—he broke his principles. His shame was so vast that as a way of atonement, he decided to leave his land and his beloved people. He jumped into a bonfire that he created and was transformed into a star. That is the first star that appears in the sky every night. From the sky, he was able to watch over his people.

For some unknown reason, the child was fascinated by the myth of Quetzalcoatl. He told his mother the story that had caused him such a strong impression. The queen, who was always interested in her child's development, was glad to hear what her son had to say.

As happy as the queen was hearing her child tell the story, she froze when her son, after finishing describing the myth, added, "Mommy, I would also like to be a star. Perhaps I could live with Quetzalcoatl in the sky! Since professor Mercedes Marin told me this myth, I have been observing the stars and they have a crown of light around them with which they seem to be comfortable. I do not see any scars in any of them." The queen kept silent. Not knowing what to say, she remarked, "I think we will have to talk about this another time. It is time for you to go to bed now. Good night, sleep tight."

The following morning, the Queen who had never before heard anything about the Myth of Quetzalcoatl, ordered to bring the Nahuatl mythology professor. When the teacher arrived, she was asked to instruct the queen about Quetzalcoatl and the myth her son had talked about. Mercedes courteously spoke about Quetzalcoatl, whose name meant "Feathered Snake." As Mercedes spoke, she was able to transmit her profound interest and admiration for her native culture. When she finished telling the myth, as the queen had asked her to do, she added, "Your majesty, I also wanted to approach you as you have asked us to do if we notice something important with your son. I have observed his special interest in this myth. He keeps asking me not only to repeat the myth, but more and more details about it. His devotion to this particular aspect of the Nahuatl mythology is outstanding. He is a brilliant and highly dedicated student of my subject. I do not have any more answers to what he seems to be looking for so I felt the need to let you know what I have observed." The queen heard the honest revelation from the professor and thanked her for the important information she had shared.

After the queen learned the information on her son and knowing herself the myth, she began observing the first star that appeared in the sky every night. Following the stars always made her think of her son wanting to become a star. As she observed the stars crowned by light, she remembered the night when there was a new moon and the first star appeared intensely shining in the sky in a particular way. Nine months after, her son was born. "Could it be possible that…" Not wanting her mind to go any further with such thoughts, the queen decided to talk to her son. As she approached him, she said, "I have been thinking about the myth you told me, I even asked your professor to tell me what interested you so deeply. I want to share with you some of my thoughts. Quetzalcoatl left his beloved people and became a star because he felt ashamed for what he did. I wonder, why would you want to become a star and be in the sky?" asked the queen. The child naively answered, "What is shame, mother?"

"Shame is," explained the queen hesitating, "a feeling we have when we do not behave in the way we should, when we behave in a wrong way." "Just as when I run all over the place and you say I shouldn't do that?" asked the child. The queen explained further, "Yes, more or less. Quetzalcoatl behaved badly. He not only broke the rules, he also failed to follow his own rules. He felt bad and decided to leave because he did not obey the rules in which he believed." The child was staring at his mother with eyes wide open. When the queen finished, the boy said, "Mommy, I also feel ashamed, like Quetzalcoatl." The queen, deeply moved, asked him, "You feel ashamed? Why my love? Why would you feel ashamed?" The child answered, "Every time my father puts the crown on my head, something hurts and I just feel like hiding forever. I want to be good, I want Father to love me, but that crown feels too heavy and my head hurts. The crown doesn't like to sit over my head. However, Father said that when I grow older, I would have to wear it more and more. He also said that the big red chair where he sits is going to be my chair. I will be in charge and take care of everybody so that there will be peace and happiness among all the people…but…I don't want that. That scares me so I behaved terrible! I ran away and hid. I don't want father to find me, I don't ever want to come out…is that what you were trying to explain to me?"

The queen, who was a sensitive and smart woman, hugged her child to comfort him. She assured him that he was a good boy, and that she, as well as his father, loved him, even after what happened. But she knew she had to talk to the king. She did not know exactly how to tell the king what she found out from their son, but she was convinced he must know. For her, there was no doubt that the boy was the most important matter in life, but now, she was not sure that it was the same for the king.

After thinking for a couple of days, the queen finally went to the king and said, "I have been observing closely our son lately because I don't perceive him to be happy. His eyes lack the sparkle that can be seen in other children and even in some adults when they are at peace in themselves…" The king interrupted, "What is it that you want to tell me?" "Well," the queen continued, "he came to me the other day to share what he had learned in his mythology class; the Myth of

Quetzalcoatl, and…" the king again, now more desperate and anxious, interrupted and said, "What is your point? Just say it!" The queen, concerned with her son's wellbeing, resumed talking. "I don't want my son to feel ashamed! I wish he did not have to hide because he is not what you expect him to be. He is only a child and he feels terrible because he thinks he is misbehaving! You want him to be the king so badly you neglect to be concerned about his happiness, it is intolerable!" The queen's voice raised and her anger was evident. "Furthermore," said the queen, "my son should not feel ashamed of who he is. He can sure shine with his own inner light in this land of yours, which since he was born has only welcomed the future king, not this child!"

The queen was silent. After what seemed a rather long pause, the king exploded with anger, "Have you gone crazy? He will be the king! Or do you now believe in children stories that some professor told our son? How can you fall for such nonsense? How is it possible that you are questioning our family's vow? Our responsibility with the continuance of our lineage, with our people, with our ancestors??!! I do not want to hear any more of this. Ah, and that professor…tell me her name because she should be thrown into exile! Out of my land, never to come back. I do not need her stories and neither does my child. I am the King, as will be my descendant!"

The king left enraged, slamming the door on his way out. The confused queen remained silent thinking of the terrible reaction she had witnessed in her husband. She had corroborated the heavy load her son had been carrying. Perhaps it was such weight that left a mark on the child's forehead when he was born—wondered the queen.

It was a long night for the queen, she felt lonely. For the first time, it was impossible to talk to her husband about a critical matter. In the following days, the child, sensing the dense energy in the environment, would hide more and more.

One night, the king had a strange dream. The dream was so intense and vivid that it drew the king's attention. He decided to call the queen to ask for her help in sorting out the impression the dream had had in him. When the queen came to him, he said, "I have to talk to you, I am somehow disturbed because of a dream I had. I want to share it with you because I am not sure what to do about it. For some reason the dream keeps coming back to me."

The king told his dream to the queen:

A strange creature appeared in our kingdom, it was a snake but it had feathers in his body. The creature managed to go into the palace. I gave the order to throw him out. He was not allowed to be in this land and certainly not in my palace. But my guards seemed to be deaf to my voice, to my orders. The feathered snake kept coming closer until he reached my throne, where I was sitting. I felt enraged! 'This is inadmissible, unprecedented. Guards!'—I screamed—'take this creature out of here!' But no one would listen to me.

The feathered snake started climbing around my body until I found myself being completely tied up. The snake was wrapped around my feet, legs, and arms until he finally reached my neck. I thought he was going to strangle me. The snake held me tight; I was suffocating. But after a while of feeling terrorized, I realized that I was still alive and unhurt. I then felt the snake's breath in my ear. In the midst of this horror, I began to hear a voice coming from that horrible being that was holding me.

To my surprise, the voice sounded human. The voice spoke in some remote and primitive language that somehow, I was able to understand. The snake spoke clearly in my ear and said: 'I understand what you are going through. You are caught in shame because of feeling at risk of betraying your principles. I have felt it myself.' 'Shame? Me? I have no shame. What would I feel ashamed of?' I answered. 'Ashamed because of the possibility of not fulfilling your duties, as well as your own expectations which you have also cherished,' said the snake. 'I am doing exactly as I ought to be doing,' I said. 'I don't know what you are talking about or who you are. I have no reason to continue listening to you.'

But the strange, feathered snake went on. 'You want to avoid feeling ashamed for failing on your promise to your ancestors and what you have sworn to yourself. You also face the possibility of failing as a father and protector of the only beloved son you were finally able to have.' 'That is not true!' I angrily yelled. 'I am the king and I am a good king. A king has a word; commitments to fulfill and also, I have my son!' And my son...my son...'

There was silence. The feathered snake, with a voice that sounded comforting, went on: 'I am a king as well so I will now talk to you as such. I have discovered that I am more human than what I thought I was, perhaps more than I even wanted. I made mistakes and I did not fulfill my own expectations. When that happened my shame was overwhelming to the point of feeling that I had to leave. I abandoned my people, my land and what I loved the most. With total lack of compassion, I felt I needed to sacrifice myself. In doing so, I sacrificed my people when they still believed in and cherished me. I came here to tell you about the cruelty I have found to be ingrained in imposed expectations of culture, religion, people, but above all by oneself. So I want to tell you that if you miss fulfilling your own demands, find atonement on this earth, in your own land, inside your heart. That way you will not need to abandon who you love the most.' As the feathered snake finished pronouncing these words, he disappeared.

The queen listened to the dream with utmost attention; she did not say a thing. Staring at the king while listening to the dream, the queen simply held his hand and finally added, "I love you, but I don't know how to help you. I only hope you can find peace in your mind and in your heart."

After having this dream, of which only the queen knew about, something did take place within the king. Even people in the kingdom talked about the change in their king. Some people said the king became weaker. Others felt that he was closer to his people. Some others thought that somehow he seemed wiser. Certainly, there were those who thought that their king had lost his track. The truth is, no one could accurately name what had happened to the king and he, as kings usually do, provided absolutely no explanation.

Years went by and both the king and the queen had aged. He became an old man always joined by his old lady. Their son, who was already married, had four beautiful children. Around that time, the king decided to build a new university. Teachers and students from all over the world, who for some reason had no access or approval in their homelands to learn what they were really interested in knowing, could come study. Courses such as archeology, mythology, various forms of art, different languages and studies about cultures were offered proving their upmost importance.

To everyone's surprise, including the queen, he named his son director of the university. The only son the king and queen were ever able to have, his yearned king to be. It was interesting to witness that when the assignation of role happened, the king was able to come close to his son, and maybe for the first time, hugged him with tears in his eyes.

While the inauguration celebration was taking place, no one really knew the tremendous sacrifice involved in the king's decision of letting his son become a university director. Only the queen knew what an act of humbleness and renunciation that meant for the king. He had always expected his son to become the king of his land and wear his dearest crown on his head. Nevertheless, for the first time in many years, the king seemed to be at peace. His face with always a contracted gesture had softened and he was even able to smile lightly.

Since then, every time the king wears his royal crown, he silently says, "Forgive me for not knowing who will be wearing you, whose head you will be crowning…I pray that you will be honored and embraced." Then he goes on conversing with the crown, "You seem to give headaches to whoever wears you, including myself. I used to be quite comfortable and proud of wearing you for many years until I realized how many things are to be considered, which I had not seen before. Perhaps in all this time of being the king and wearing you, dear crown, I am beginning to wonder, for what reason were you really created? You have sat on top of my head for so many years during which, both your shine and your weight, have colored my vision of the world. I had no other way to understand life, other than under the light you shed. After so many years of wearing you, I now wonder, can anyone wear you without losing one's unique opportunity and privilege to own one's unique life? By being terribly attractive, absolutely demanding and dangerously convincing, you can make one feel nothing more than a king. How poor can one get to live when falling under your absolute spell." While the king spoke, there, sat the crown, right on his hands, lavishly shining as it always did.

Years went by and the king went on honestly trying to rule his kingdom as wise and fair as he could. Getting really old, the king was nearing death. One day, while lying on his bed, his youngest granddaughter came to visit him. She knocked on the door and said, "Hi Grandpa, it is me, may I come in?" Hearing the voice of his beloved granddaughter, the king answered, "Of course come in Sweetheart."

"Hello Grandpa, I wanted to come visit with you. I especially wanted to come today because I heard my father say that you are going to go to the sky soon, is that right Grandpa?"

"That is right Sweetie. Soon I will be leaving to the sky."

"And how are you going to go to the sky Grandpa?"

"I have been thinking about it myself and I remembered, I have a friend who has helped me do hard work other times in my life. He has a lot of feathers on his body; perhaps he even knows how to fly. I know he can certainly hold me tight without hurting me a bit. I have already seen that before. Probably he will be the one taking me to the sky."

"And when you live in the sky, can I come visit? How will I see you then Grandpa?"

"When the stars come out at night, you should know, I will be one of them. I will be watching and taking care of you from the sky."

"Will that be possible because of your crown Grandpa? Your crown sure looks like a starred sky. Will you be wearing it in the sky?"

"No, I will not take my crown with me. It is too heavy to travel with and to move around, I found that out later in my life."

"Oh, but it is so beautiful and you like it so much and so do I... mmmm...you think maybe I can try it on?"

"You sure can, but be careful Sweetheart because wearing a crown for too long often brings headaches."

"Why would that be Grandpa? I have never felt a headache when I play and do the things I like. I am only going to try it on for a little while to play with it...let's see how it feels."

The king, still faithful to his crown, looked at his granddaughter with wide eyes and said, "Wearing a crown is a serious matter—it is not a game, you should know that."

"I am sorry Grandpa, I didn't mean to upset you. If the crown is so heavy that it can give you a headache, I wouldn't want it to stop me from playing other games I love to play, I would be very bored."

As the king heard his granddaughter, he smiled and said, "Let's see how it feels if you are to wear it, go ahead, try it on."

The girl carefully placed the crown on her head. As the king watched the crown he had been wearing for so many years being placed over the girl's head by her own little hands, he thought, "It sure is big. It always has been so, even for myself…but also very beautiful indeed…perhaps one day it may really fit her…"

The girl went on talking as she felt the crown sitting on her head, "Grandpa, Father says I have a very big head…so…Oh! Look Grandpa, you see, it doesn't look that big, does it? See how gorgeous it is! And it feels fine! Do you think I look like you Grandpa? Grandpa? Grandpa…"

"It seems that Grandpa fell asleep," said the girl. Perhaps he needs to take a nap if he is going to go out and play with his feathered friend. I should let him sleep. He might reach the sky tonight." Before leaving, she climbed up to the royal bed where the king was peacefully lying with a smile on his face, she gave the king a kiss goodbye and said, "See you later Grandpa, sleep tight and oh, if you get to go to the sky, don't forget to blink, I will be watching you from here every night. Love you."

SHOWERS

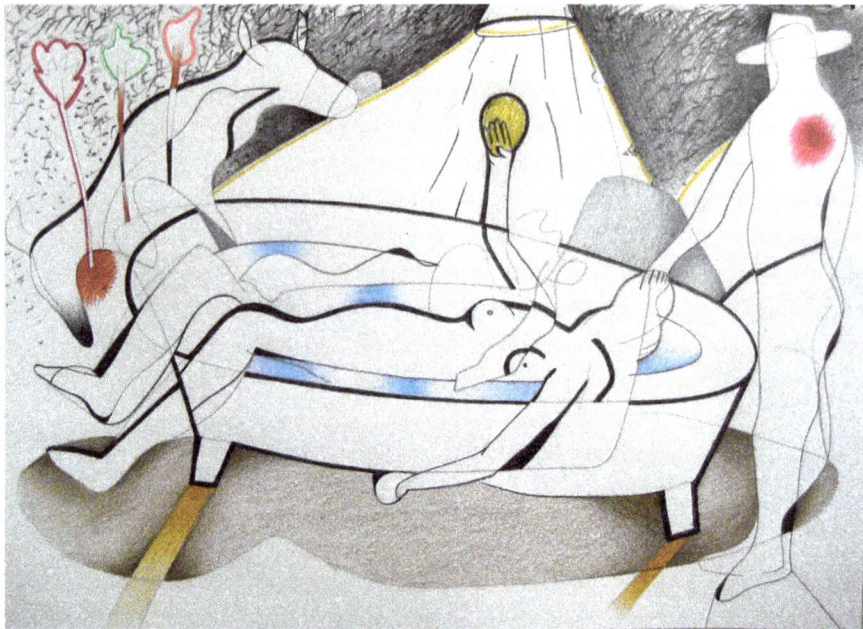

Refreshing and profoundly enlivening are the baths provided by the vast fountainhead, where pristine water is still able to arise in a remote corner of the earth. People from all places throughout the globe are for some reason willing to travel for days and days to come here, which requires crossing arid territories with nearly total lack of comfort, and long periods of rationed water and food, to be able to access this special place in the world called the Water House. It receives such name, because this is where the most special baths take place.

From what we have heard, people who come to this place to experience a moistening of body and soul that will release a smooth flow of healing energy in their lives, seem to be usually satisfied. The place was known for being able to please the most difficult people, in situations that have strong exigencies. Baths of all types are available—from submerging oneself into the precious liquid having the precise temperature, into which all kinds of salts, as well as different herbs with specific attributes and even flower petals are added, all the way to the experience of being surrounded by warm steam into which fragrances that enhance the senses have been included. The softening and nourishing of all skin types is in this way accomplished through the soothing delivery of water. There is even the possibility of inhaling the steam arising from bubbling water so that respiratory tracts can be cleaned as well. For this purpose, purifying and refreshing tree leaves have been volatilized within the steam. There is also the simplest way of feeling immersed in nature: swimming in the small river created from the emerging waters. One can gently propel oneself in the midst of beautiful trees and greenery, which can create a magnificent stage for the communion with nature that occurs in this special scenery.

But the specialty of this place is to be found where, set apart from all these other exquisite possibilities of experiencing the healing magic of water, are the showers. These showers are special not only for the different settings in which they are built, but because they are unique to each person's need of seeking this particular form of attention. An important aspect is the way these showers allow contact with the precious liquid, mirroring the flowing stream of life and the possibility of renewal. And apparently, during this casual daily act in most people's life, all sorts of stories appeared…

Expert workers, who for many years had been doing this job, would meet the people from different backgrounds who came to the Water House. Experience had taught these workers how to see the depth of the people's need, which brought them to this special place with such difficult journey.

At one time, a two-and-a-half-year-old girl was brought to the Water House. Her father was a renowned physician, and her mother, a professional nurse. They had long been reluctant to take their daughter anywhere that did not have scientifically proven credentials. But none of these places had been able to help their daughter. The girl was chronically dehydrated and had recently begun to develop anemia. The reason was that she could not stop vomiting. This worrisome symptom of seemingly endless stream of vomit usually began just before the little girl's evening bath, until she was dirty, dehydrated, and exhausted. This situation, which no regular medicine had been able to resolve, had physically and emotionally exhausted the resources of the family, to the point that the parents were finally ready to go beyond their usual skepticism in search for a solution.

After hearing the predicament that had overtaken this family, the experts at the Water House suggested in the most casual way, that in order to experience the sort of treatment their daughter would get, both parents bathe first in special baths that would be prepared for them. "What a ridiculous demand!" thought the parents, but they did not refuse. In fact, they were even able to laugh appreciatively at the simplicity of the suggestion.

A bath was indeed prepared for the little girl's parents, in which, as expected, they had absolutely no say in the matter. This was in fact the first time in many years they had not been allowed to investigate and decide, but to allow themselves to experience the unexpected. In their baths, they oscillated between iced water, to really steamy hot baths, where new elements were constantly being introduced: rare herbs, flower petals, unknown soaps; there were also showers of all sorts of volume, intensity, and speed to be incorporated in each day. Perhaps the one thing the baths and the showers had in common was the awakening of the senses—they were the most pleasurable and sensual baths one could ever have dreamed taking. At the end of their experience, the parents were totally ready to offer their daughter her bath. The staff had told them, it was very important that they handle her bathing.

And so, the same practice went on—bathing was first offered to the parents, then by the parents to their child. It went along at first without enthusiasm, because by now, there was little hope that nothing could ever make her feel better. But the day arrived when the little girl, despite her usual vomiting, after finishing her long and carefully administered bath, was warmly and compassionately hugged by her parents. For once, she was not measured by her therapeutic progress. She was not scolded for continuing to manifest her inevitable and annoying symptom of vomiting, but was hugged and held with the same love that had gone into bathing her. Her parents simply hugged her warmly, which seemed to be a long enough hug that they began sweating, and then a kind of miracle happened. They started sweating away an invisible layer of frozen skin that had been holding them in its grip like ice for more years than they could possibly count. Since there was no precedent in any science they knew for such an outcome, for the first time in their adult lives they forgot about scientific diagnosis altogether, and this new unexpected flexibility allowed themselves to tell their daughter, "Sweetheart, we are here for you, we love you, we won't ever leave you, everything is going to be fine."

From then on, talking with the little girl and hugging her after the special washings had taken place became a regular part of this little girl's bath. She enjoyed it so much that after a while she even seemed to forget the vomiting. So incredulous were the parents that their scientific curiosity resurfaced and they approached the Water House experts with a very serious questioning look on their faces, saying they wanted to analyze the case with them for the benefit of future families in such a situation. They did indeed get an answer, but not the one they were expecting. "The case?" What case? Your little girl is not 'a case,' she is your daughter." The parents remained quiet, but they did not budge in their commitment to the duty they felt to all the world's parents. Jaw firmly set, the mother went on, "We need to know what this has been about. What has been learned here, we need to understand it, for us, for our daughter, for other children!"

Carefully, the Water House experts responded, "We can try to give you an answer that we think applies to your daughter. We have been thinking that your daughter's endless vomiting has been her attempt to extrude from her system, a void that she feels and finds intolerable. We think this void was from lack of being held by you and seen as your precious and unique daughter; the lack of any feeling of joy from you towards her developing ability to be the person she is, instead of fulfilling the measure of awaited achievements. She could not do anything except of course the wise decision her body was making to keep on vomiting that emptiness out. After what you have experienced here, we don't think it is necessary to tell you, that you have expressed your love and pride towards her for who she is, as innocent of demand as the day she was born…"

The Water House experts stopped talking when they saw the parents' faces. Nothing else was said until finally the father broke the clearly aroused tension and said, "This has certainly been one more unexpected and very cold shower…this time, with words…" he took a deep breath and then went on, "I don't know how much my actual cells can incorporate what I am hearing, because…I should say…in my scientific words, that my DNA seems to carry a different code for understanding processes in life than what was just said…but nevertheless…I can admit, that was one more refreshing shower, all the more remarkable because it was a shower of ideas we had not previously allowed to touch us." Then the mother picked up the conversation and with deep courage dared to say, "I believe my husband is right. We came here with a dehydrated girl, and now I think that we were the ones in need of refreshing. Our very long ago inherited DNA needed to be moistened. We didn't know that it had dried out." Then, as if talking to herself, she went on, "You know that 'dehydration in the flow of ideas' and 'creativity anemia' have often overtaken us. Those symptoms have been our long feared ghosts, threatening our personal and professional lives. In fact it was that specific and deeply ingrained fear we have of succumbing to them that we saw getting lived out by our daughter." She looked at her husband and then said, "The only real news is you and I have work to do, but we are hard workers, we have always been, and will do it. We won't let our daughter dry out again because we are afraid to avail ourselves of the moistening we need."

The day arrived when the family returned home. However, the bathing experts also learned something from that experience. After years of practicing this work, they had finally realized that the people arriving, were always seeking something that was not yet clear, even to themselves, and so they were unlikely able to name it.

After this had become clear to the staff, among the people that arrived, there was once a young man who came announcing he was there because he did not want to take a bath at all. He completely refused to have any contact with running water. To be sure, when he arrived, it was difficult to come physically close to him since his odor was so strong, but the staff realized that was nothing other than the most evident manifestation of a statement, the basis of which, at that moment was totally incomprehensible to them.

Nevertheless, with upmost respect, he was asked the usual question as to the reason that had brought him to the Water House. The young man answered, "I have not taken a bath in a very long time, I have not wanted to, in fact, I completely try to avoid any bathing because I feel fine with the way I am." This gave the experts a chance to ask the obvious question, "Then why did you decide to come to the Water House?" To which the young man had an interesting answer, "The reason for coming here at this point of my life is that my skin has begun to itch, and since you are known for having every kind of baths, I came to see if perhaps there would be some special one that is good for itching." The experts listening to his response took this opportunity to ask what was really confusing them. "Before we get to that, would you mind telling us why is it that you don't like taking baths?"

"I think it is too long of a story for me to tell in full, you wouldn't want to hear it. It goes all the way back to my very early years in life." Rather quickly, the young man received another response from the experts. "We do want to hear it and it's okay to take your time." Getting ready to tell a very old history, he took a deep breath and began talking. "I will try to make it as brief as possible. It is not so pleasant, you know, since I can remember everything I ever had, even though much was taken away from me. When I was very young, my food was taken from my hands because I was so messy. Later, when I grew up, I had a rock collection, which was my treasure. I used to hide it because I had already sensed the sort of situation in which I had to survive. I knew that my beautiful rocks were not really clean since I had picked them off the ground when playing outdoors. I thought I had hidden them cleverly in our house where my mother could not find them, but as she had a nose for any "dirt" of mine, she did find my magnificent collection of special rocks and threw them away. They did not belong to the perfect house she wanted to keep, and she did not want them around. And as for my father, every time I shared any thoughts with him, my very tender ideas were disposed of as immature, since it was clear that he was the only man in the house old enough to be right. So you see, I grew up knowing that I just couldn't have anything that I wanted to make my own—not my food, not my rocks, not my ideas, and of course, not even my feelings! They were not for me to cultivate in order to flourish, as far as my parents were concerned. In their eyes, I was not bright enough to know what was expected of me. Do you understand?" asked the young man—continuing so fast there was no time for the experts to answer him. "As I grew up, the most common word I heard was No, you don't do that, you don't behave like that, you don't speak such things, that's not the way you are supposed to feel. My entire childhood was one long—No.

One day in the midst of profound sadness, I simply stopped bathing myself. I just was not interested in life anymore. What was the point of a bath when I was losing my will to live? One day, after several nights of running the water but never getting in the tub, I woke up to discover that for the first time in my life, there was a rather strange and intense odor emanating from me. I'm not saying I liked it but it was mine and mine alone. It was one thing I had that was safe, because even though my newfound odor was severely criticized, as was the rest of myself, no one was able to take it away from me. It was then that I began stinking, but that was no more nor less than I have felt all my life anyway. Even when I used to bathe, it felt I stank as a person. So that was why, since then I refused bathing…until now, when I have begun to itch."

After carefully hearing the young man's account, one of the Water House experts said, "Well, I hope we are able to find something that suits your need to stop itching." It took some days to figure out a possible way to ease the young man's itching, for they knew that sooner or later it would require soap and water, which for now was not an option. Some time passed and still stinking, this young man was approached by the experts. They asked him directly if he would help them design showers for their other clients. One of the experts explained, "People with various needs come here to bathe, so we like to offer many possibilities according to their personal needs. So, my colleagues and I thought that, knowing how particular are the needs people who come here can have, maybe you would like to help us design the showers for them." "Well," said the young man, "if you don't mind my odor, I will…although I don't know if I can be of any help because I lack…" He was then interrupted by one of the experts who said, "Okay, give it a try, we'll see you early tomorrow morning. We prefer doing that work at the garden level, right in front of the oak tree, and we will meet you there." Nothing else was said.

The next morning, with his usual strong emanating odor, the young man arrived to work at the Shower Design Workshop. And so he did, day after day, until the time arrived that having participated in this creative task, he wanted to try for himself how the newly designed showers worked. He wanted to find out how people would feel taking them, especially the ones who didn't find bathing so easy to accept, even with a specially designed bathing experience. Though still ambivalent about taking a shower, he approached the experts, and said, "I have been thinking, I would like to try the new shower that we finished last week, only to see how it works, nothing else, and it will be very, very fast, and I will not…" Again, he was interrupted with a short answer, "If you feel like trying it, I guess that is the right thing to do." Hearing this answer he went further, "Would it be okay if…well, perhaps tomorrow morning, or maybe…" but in his seemingly endless apology for every word that came out of his mouth to express what he wanted, he got to hear, "You can do it any day you want, as long as it is early morning before we start working, got it?" "Oh yes, yes of course," the young man answered.

And so it was how this young man who did not want to lose the only one thing he had ever been able to keep to himself without it being torn away from him with searing criticism and rejection—his strong odor—the very same thing that gave him not only the recent itching, but for far longer, a sense of existence, did take a bath early one morning using a water shower he himself had helped to design and develop. That particular shower was intended for sensitive people who would rather experience a light spray of warm water than a dense, thick, spurt of endlessly running hot water under which it was, in the young man's words, "like drowning, it was impossible to defend oneself from."

After that special bathing experience, his itching diminished considerably, but even more important, so did his fear. Consequently, he was able to give up his very strong odor. From then, he was committed, as a shower artist, to contributing to the design and manufacture of different kinds of bathing, and he became recognized for his great subtlety in the creation of showers. This young man who could formerly only own his strong odor, was for the first time able to feel the pride at participating in the creation of something new. So gifted was he in this matter, that no one like him was able to see with so much subtleness, how showers could respond to the most varied and demanding sensitivities.

While these developments were taking place in the Shower Design Workshop, one day, a lady arrived at the Water House who looked so very tired that it was difficult to know her age. She didn't speak much, and when she was addressed with the regular question placed to all people arriving to this place, "How can we help you?" Her answer was, "I don't know if you *can* help me, I am here only because I don't have anywhere to go." With such a response, no matter the very many responses the staff had heard before, the experts at the Water House were quite surprised. Nevertheless, they went on asking with the usual care they took towards anyone, "In order to fulfill our duty, we would like to know why you are here." The woman kept silent for a long time, practically expressionless, until finally she resumed talking, "I am here because I heard that your showers have the benefit of renewal." That is all she said, then once again there was silence.

Hearing this, the staff, even though they had begun feeling at a loss with the woman, asked again, "May we inquire why renewal would be important for you? Would you mind telling us perhaps a bit of your story so that we are able to respond?" To which the woman bitterly answered, "I will think about it and let you know when I have an answer."

And so it was, for many days and even weeks, the woman quietly observed the exchanges that went on at the Water House. The people who arrived were somehow different when they left, more satisfied than before. In this way she experienced the results of what she was unable to decipher. She got to watch the experts, the same ones who, the very first day she arrived asked her questions she didn't want to answer. She needed to prove for herself how and why they did the job they had chosen. Before she could tell them anything, she wanted to make sure that they were not only capable, but also careful and compassionate; that they have a heart to hear with, and a head to respond to what she had to say. She wanted to be able to trust, but in her case, she deeply doubted that would ever be possible. As she observed the staff, she thought to herself, "Where is this all going to take me now?"

One gray foggy morning, she called upon one of the staff members who received her the very first day she arrived; the one member who did not ask her any questions and nevertheless was fully present.

"I will answer you now," said the woman in a most sudden and almost unexpected way. "I am here because when I shower I don't get wet." She then paused. Catching her breath, she went on, "It is only on the surface that water seems to run over my hair and my skin, because when I brush my hair, I realize that underneath it is dry, it never gets wet, and so is my body. The splashing water won't touch my skin, and everything in me and around me stays dry."

The expert at the Water House who was listening to her noticed that there was a slight opening to communicate with her and she then said, "I understand you don't like to be questioned, and I respect it, but whenever you are ready to speak, if you decide it is convenient for you, may I know how long this has been going on?" In that same moment, surprisingly, the woman began talking.

"I was once under a shower, where I was supposed to be in order to take a bath…" she interrupted, "by the way, I should say, there was a time in my life when I enjoyed very much taking my shower…that was a very long time ago, it seems to correspond to another life…but that particular time, when I was forced to stand under the shower, I suddenly looked up and saw that it had a strange shape, one I had never seen before. Then I was able to perceive a strange odor…and soon after, I began feeling intoxicated by what was coming out of the shower, which kept intensifying more and more. I began coughing, I wanted to take it out of my system, but I couldn't, sooner than later, it had penetrated through every opened pore in my skin. I fight it! I fight it with every bit of life's energy I had, but I just couldn't avoid it. Suddenly, as I was falling, it stopped completely. The poisonous gas had run out. There, standing under that shower, I realized, I had miraculously remained alive.

After these words were pronounced, there was a long silence. Neither one of the two participants was able to say anything further. Soon after the woman had confessed her story, she felt so uncomfortable and ashamed, that she began apologizing, as if she would be really guilty— guilty of having spoken, guilty of remaining alive, guilty of being there looking for help, guilty for wanting to go on living. In the middle of what amounted to her begging forgiveness, the Water House expert, without any further questions wholeheartedly said, "There is nothing to apologize about, I am glad you are here, and that I have met you. Thank you for sharing your story. I can assure you, we will honor it." By then, the face of the woman who had just confessed her deepest, most shameful secret had returned to its usual lack of expression.

Days, perhaps weeks or even months passed after this most intense conversation had taken place, and in fact, for the woman, the chronologic measuring of time had lost its meaning. Living close to nature itself had apparently allowed her to find her own inner feminine nature, for the woman realized within her very own body how cycles take place in a world that is ever-changing.

The Water House expert and the woman became friends and they talked often about different topics. One day, the expert addressed the woman with the unexpected proposal that had been waiting to be offered since the very first day she arrived. "Today your shower is ready." The woman's immediate response of panic was unavoidable. In shock, her face contracted, her unblinking eyes flew wide open, and her mouth tightly closed like it would never open again. Her shoulders closed in and her back became bent, but nevertheless, she walked together with her trusted friend to where she had once only pointed. Being in a space surrounded by walls with open ceiling, she very soon saw an unknown shower placed high on one of the walls, under which she was to stand up, and so she did. Under such intensity, all possible horrifying images filled her mind, her soul, and spirit. In that precise moment when she felt she was really going to die, butterflies began to come out of the shower above her head. Yes, it is true. Flying butterflies came out from the strange shower under which she was standing, hundreds of them flying free under the shining sun, into an endless blue sky.

Tears began rolling down the woman's face, reaching her neck, followed by unaccountable more tears which went on rolling down her clothing, her body, and suddenly, she became wet, once again.

It is in that special corner of the world, known to some as the Water House, which even now continues to exist for anyone seeking a truly different way to relate to the flow of life, offering a place where one can arrive in order to explore, discover, and finally find some unexpected new possibility. There, for such a seeker, is a shower on order, created to suit that individual's deepest and unique needs.

WISSEY

Once upon a time in a remote and recently discovered land there was a mother of a strange species who was about to give birth to her babies. The delivery was not easy. The first two babies were born in quick succession, both robust and healthy. However, while the mother was still recovering from the delivery, a third one came out. This one was not in the best condition and unfortunately did not survive. The birthing process appeared to have ended, when unexpectedly a fourth one appeared, the tiniest of them all, but nevertheless, just the cutest little thing. The mother was so busy attending to the first two babies and so distressed at the loss of the third one that she almost forgot she had another baby.

The runt of the litter, this little fourth one, whom I will call Wissey, somehow managed to get a few drops of milk that were left after the other two had finished feeding. Surviving was not really a problem while her littermates were around, but pretty soon she found herself completely alone. All the others had left, even the mother, who, having done her duty, went off to resume her former life. Tiny Wissey, who had become accustomed to filling up her stomach on leftover drops of milk, was able to survive on almost anything that she could find to eat. It was not so much the scarcity of actual food that bothered her, but the lack of emotional nourishment and the cold, empty feeling in her heart.

It was in such bleak circumstances that Wissey was forced to survive. To her good fortune, soon enough, a little girl passed by her lonely nest. "Oh, what a pretty little creature!" said the girl. "Is it a puppy? It's so tiny that it's hard to tell. Oh, I would love to have a dog! I don't have any friends, and a dog would be so much fun to play with." When Wissey heard the child saying that she would "love" to have a dog, she pricked up her ears. "Here's my chance," she said to herself, "I just found what I've been looking for. I could serve as a dog for this dear little child and then I will be cherished and loved. I just need to bark and wag my tail and behave like a dog, and she will love me in return." So Wissey, with her tiny little voice, which had just begun to make audible sounds, barked as loudly as she could and wagged her tail, as if she were a real dog.

The girl began playing with Wissey, and as she did, Wissey instantly felt the love pouring out of her heart. The girl petted, hugged, and kissed Wissey so profusely that the people passing by marveled at how spontaneously children give love, so freely and in such an unrestrained manner. And this was clearly felt by Wissey too. Her heart was finally being nurtured as she was cared for and embraced for the first time in her life. The coldness that had enveloped her heart melted away with the warmth of love the girl was giving her, and she began licking the girl's face. Delighted with her lucky find, the girl ran home to show her family her new dog.

But as is the case with every paradise, this one was not meant to last forever. Another creature inserted itself into this idyllic scene in the form of the girl's older sister. Driven by jealousy, the sister announced that she didn't want to have a dog in their home. "Dogs," she declared, "have only one master, and since I am the eldest child in the family, I deserve that role." In reality, however, she could not hold that privileged position with regard to Wissey, since she was incapable of expressing the kind of love that her younger sister gave the tiny creature. Knowing that she could not replicate the amazingly close relationship between her younger sister and Wissey, she insisted that she just wouldn't accept having a dog. "If we are to have a pet," she decreed, "it should be a cat. Cats adopt human families, and perhaps a cat might even adopt me as its favorite family member. But I certainly will not have a dog that barks and wags its tail and jumps with joy only when my sister appears."

Hearing this, Wissey fell into a panic. In order to protect herself against this threat to her innermost self, she curled up into a ball in an attempt to keep out the coldness that she once again felt creeping into her heart. Thus she remained, in a state of paralyzed terror, until she was awakened by the excited cries of the little girl. The girl was saying: "Oh, no, no! Come see what's happened to Wissey's coat. It's changed. I can't believe it—she looks really different! Take a look! I think we made a mistake. Look carefully. Wissey's not a dog; she's a cat! There's no doubt she's a cat. She was so very tiny when I brought her home that we all mistook her for a puppy, when in reality, she's a little kitten!"

Wissey looked up into the girl's loving eyes and saw in them a look that only those in a deeply truthful relationship can share, where words are not needed for understanding one another, and in that moment,

Wissey started to mew. "Meow! Meow! Meow! Meow!" was heard all over the house as Wissey started behaving like a cat, realizing that being a cat was the only way to save herself and survive at this new turn of events.

So, having begun by barking like a dog when she first felt the spark of love from the little girl, Wissey now needed not only to be like a cat, but also to relate to the whole family, difficult as that was, in this new role. Hardest of all, she had to hide her love for the one person who had been her savior at the most precarious moment of her life, and had come to her rescue once again, but had somehow to distance herself from her in order to protect her.

For a while, this new arrangement brought peace into Wissey's world and she was able to remain with the people she knew. Once in a while, with her tail, as cats usually do, she would casually caress the girl who had saved her life more than once. The child would of course reciprocate but carefully and discretely, so that no one would notice the deep meaning of their relationship.

One day, the girl's father came storming into the house, and Wissey, as soon as she saw him, ran away and hid, for the father, in a fit of rage, began screaming, "I am sick and tired of having to do all the work by myself to support this family while everyone else is just having fun. I have to carry wood all day long so that all of you can have something to eat. I even have to feed that cat, who seems to be here only to eat!" From her hiding place, Wissey heard these words and was paralyzed with fear. Once again she felt her existence threatened. She remained absolutely still, quiet, and unseen.

But once again, her beloved friend came to her aid. That sweet girl, from the very first moment she heard her father's tirade, sensed the danger that was threatening Wissey and immediately began thinking about how to save her. This time it would be much more difficult than when her sister had objected. As she racked her brains for a solution, she began looking for Wissey in all the usual places she loved, but there was no sign of her dear friend.

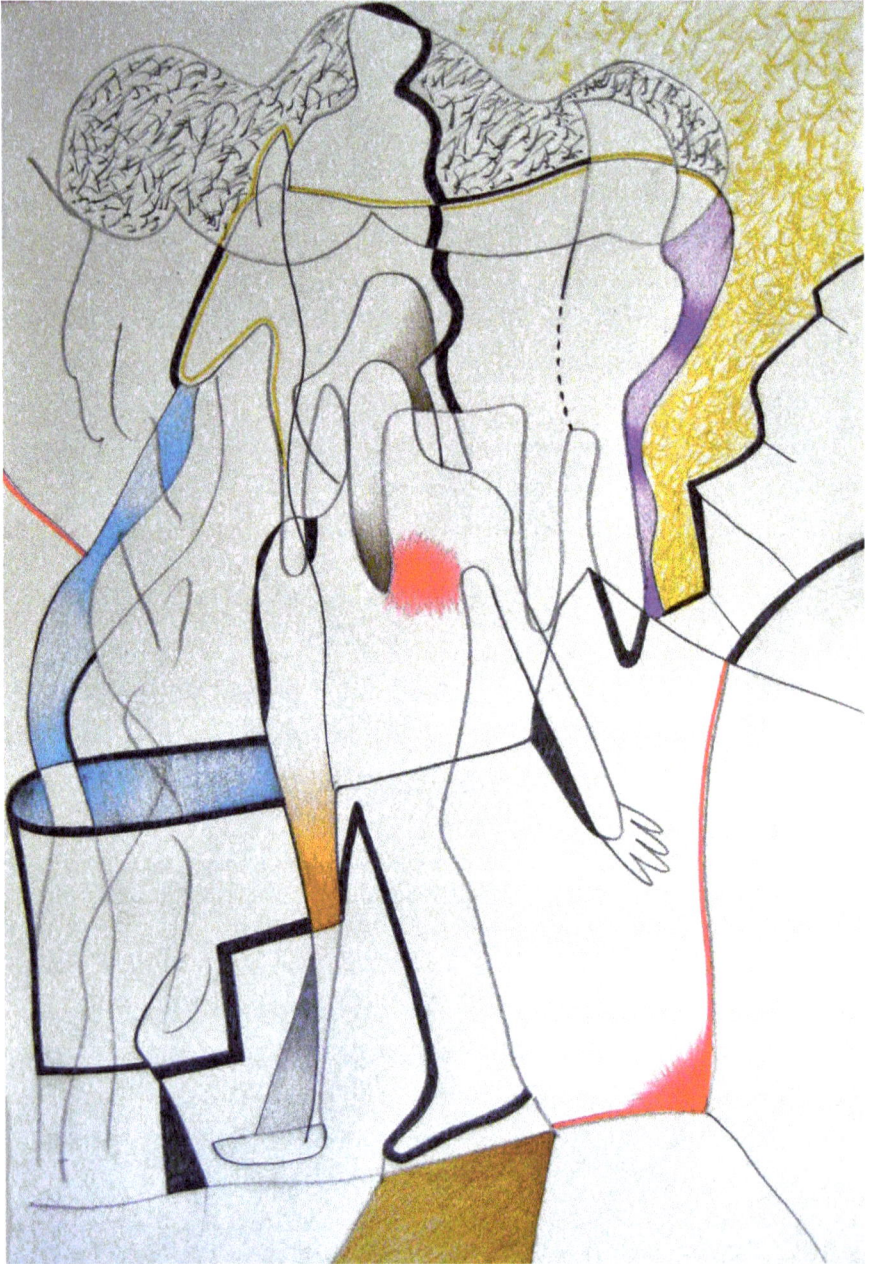

"She must have been really scared," thought the child, "to disappear without a trace." The girl was about to give up when she spotted the tip of Wissey's tail twitching among the shadows in the dark corner where the cat was hiding. Knowing how scared Wissey must have been feeling, she began murmuring her name gently as she approached the terrified creature.

"Oh, dear Wissey! I thought I'd lost you. I've missed you so much! I love you so very dearly. I would do anything for you to be with me. Please come out and play with me. You are my very best friend. You know I'd never hurt you. Please, come to me." Wissey heard the familiar voice, the voice of love that had helped her survive in the past. Reassured, she came out, reluctantly at first, but then with greater confidence. Joyfully and lovingly, they played together, remembering what it was like to have one another.

So absorbed were the two friends in playing that they did not notice the father approaching. He appeared quite suddenly and spotted the cat. "There you are!" he roared. "The missing one, for whom I sweat all day long! Whoever invited you to be part of this family? You, who just gives me more work to do, I've a good mind to get rid of you!" Utterly humiliated and terrified by these cruel words, Wissey wished she could just disappear from the face of the earth. She tried to crawl back into her hiding place, never to come out again, never to be seen again, and especially never to experience again the existential anguish that had made her wish she had never been born.

Aware of Wissey's deep humiliation, and in great distress herself, the girl collected her wits quickly, looked up at her father, and said calmly: "Hello, father. I didn't notice you coming in. Guess what Wissey and I have been talking about. Can you see how big Wissey has grown? How strong she is? We've been thinking that…well…you know, Wissey's so big now, she even looks like a small donkey, don't you think? See, her ears are pointing up, and her coat has grown so thick that I've been thinking…perhaps…you know, Wissey could earn her keep by helping you carry the wood that you've been carrying on your own all this time. If she can help you, then can she stay so I will have someone to play with? She won't bother you at all, I promise. Please say yes."

As she heard these words, Wissey's beautiful round eyes filled with tears. She turned to look at the girl. Their eyes met once again, this time in tacit understanding, for they both knew that at this juncture the only way for her to survive was to be a donkey.

So from that day on, Wissey served as a donkey, carrying loads for the girl's father. The harder she worked to justify her existence, the stronger she became on the outside. Paradoxically, however, she felt an increasing coldness in her heart.

Time passed, and afraid of losing her only source of love and belonging, Wissey went on being a donkey. Taking advantage of her meekness and obedience, the father made her loads bigger and forced her to work longer hours. Her beautiful fur began to fall out and the bare patches on her skin developed hard calluses. Eventually, she lost her entire coat, and her skin covered with calluses got to be as thick and cumbersome as an elephant's hide. Her legs could hardly bear the weight of the heavy loads she had to carry, but there was no other option than to go on working, until one day, on her way back home, the weight of her load added to that of her own heavily callused skin got to be so great that she just fell to the ground and could not get up again.

When Wissey did not return home that night, the girl went to bed with a heavy heart, hoping that she would turn up the next morning, but she did not. Several days went by and there was still no sign of Wissey. The girl looked everywhere for her, in every corner that she could think of, and even on the road where Wissey carried her loads, but she simply could not find her. She cried for nights and days, longing for the only true friend she had ever known.

As for Wissey, for the second time in her life she was utterly on her own. She spent long, dark, fearful nights confronting the one thing she had been running away from since she was born—being alone. The only thing that accompanied her heart was the memory of the love she had received so consistently from the girl who rescued her when she was first abandoned, who had embraced her and remained her friend through thick and thin. Keeping this memory in her mind, in her heart, in her soul, Wissey realized that she was alive, that she had continued existing even though she was utterly alone.

"Who keeps this memory if not me?" thought Wissey in her solitude. "Where is it held so that I can still get to feel the warmth running in my veins? When I think of the girl, my heart begins to pound." Realizing that she was still alive, Wissey started wondering, "Can it really be true that I can exist on my own without feeling threatened? Without needing to be what I am not—a dog, a cat, a donkey? Without feeling obliged to meet the expectations and demands of others? And yet, as I embrace the memory of the one girl who really loved me, just that one person in the world, I feel embraced myself."

Then there was a pause. A long, still pause that lasted for what seemed like an eternity. No one could see what was taking place under that thick, hardened outer layer of skin. One might even have concluded that Wissey, exhausted from the effort of fulfilling duties and expectations in a life that was not her own, had finally died.

Years passed, and the little girl who had once adopted Wissey and loved her so deeply, grew up into a lovely but lonely woman. From time to time, she would go out into the woods, still harboring the hope that she would one day find Wissey. She just could not accept her father's suggestion that Wissey must have run away to avoid the hard work.

One day, as she was walking along in her unyielding search for her lost friend, she spotted something lying on the ground that reminded her of Wissey's hardened, callused skin. She ran towards it in the love-inspired hope of finding at last her long-lost beloved friend. It was indeed Wissey's skin—only it was just the skin she found with nothing inside it. It was an empty shell, a discarded cocoon. Amazed, she picked it up, as she had picked Wissey up so many times before, to caress her. And as she did so, a piece of paper fell out from inside it. There, on that tiny scrap of paper, written in the most beautiful handwriting, was a brief message. It read:

Forever grateful,
  Wissey

SAVORING

In one of the far away corners of the world, inhabited mostly by sun and sand, there was a small community of people who lived in the midst of enormous difficulties. It was a huge desert in which one could only see piled up sand, forming soft, round curves thus creating an unforgettable landscape, where people lived a constant challenge to survive with the small amount of water they were able to get from a faraway well. That was their only source of precious liquid, but it had served them for many generations. They believed the gods had assigned them the task of living in that specific place no matter how adverse its condition.

A time arrived when the prince of that small community reached the age of marriage. His father, a wise old king who was still ruling over the people who had chosen to remain in that ancient, mostly dry place, advised his son to go out into the world and look for a wife. He also advised his son that it was time to move on and find a more amiable place for his own descendants where they could grow up and water was abundant. Though reluctant about leaving not only his father and beloved people, but also the place he had always known, the prince still understood his father.

The day to leave home soon arrived, and with deep gratitude, the prince said goodbye to his parents. He was grateful to them not only for having raised him in such a loving way, but because they were now ready to sacrifice the love they felt to their child in favor of his future wellbeing. They had realized that he had to leave his hometown not to come back. After a deeply felt farewell, the prince left the desert kingdom.

He traveled to the north, where the well that had provided his father's people with water had been for years and years. For the last time, the prince looked at the spot where he had previously visited many times, always with good feeling that he would get the precious liquid his countrymen needed. This time, when he saw the well, it gave him confidence that he would be able to find what he is looking for: not only a wife, but a good place to settle where he could raise a new family and honor his parents wishes for him.

He traveled further for days and days until he arrived at a place where he saw different types of trees and plants, all of them green. It had large extensions of grass, so very green, fresh and moist that he found it hard to believe what his eyes were seeing. "I never thought something this moist could exist," he said to himself, "I don't think I have to go any further, this is life itself and it is magnificent!" With the excitement of having found an oasis that until then had only existed as a fantasy, he decided to look for a place where he could stay overnight and hopefully be able to remain.

This turned out to be easy to do. Gradually, he organized himself to have a life in this place that had shown him the prospect of a totally new possibility of living. At first, the other people who were there simply let him explore. Eventually, he met a beautiful young woman, modest but friendly, who had been raised on a small farm where the sweetest fruits and most delicious vegetables were grown. He had already heard of her. Because of her charm and zest, the people of this place called her the "Princess of the Meadow." He found it easy to meet her in a most casual way, and she was intrigued to encounter a man with such refined and noble manners. She was surprised to learn that he came from a land where there was practically no water and as a consequence, the earth was unable to offer its richness. The prince was utterly charmed by the ease of this woman who was so ready to take in what he had to tell her, and who was as sweet and moist as the very same fruit he was learning to enjoy in this new piece of earth that he had discovered.

To one's surprise, they eventually decided to marry. When the newly united couple had to decide where to establish their home, they both preferred to stay close to the very same place that he had so recently discovered. It was near the very same farm she had lived in and loved all her of life. Travelling just a bit farther north, they arrived at a small town that had been built right by the ocean. Like the farm, it had a natural garden, with lots of green areas, but it had an additional magnificence—a huge, seemingly endless expanse of water, which in the far off distance united with the sky overhead. The water, on one of its sides, was framed by golden sand. It was in sight of this vision, which happened to be real, that the couple decided they would establish their home.

With the luck strong believers have when they find themselves in reach of what they so much want, they were able to find a small cozy home, already built, which had the very view they had discovered the day they had come upon this charming setting. They moved into their new home and soon enough were making their lives in this idyllic place.

One late afternoon as they sat together watching the sunset from their little terrace facing the ocean, each of them savoring a hot cup of tea, they quietly rejoiced at the sky turning shades of orange as the sun was beginning to hide right where it met with the ocean. Just then, watching the beauty ingrained in this natural phenomenon, the prince remembered the severe dryness of his place of origin, and how difficult it had been to get even a single drop of water. Tears rolled down his face. "After all, there is water," he thought, "the most precious and desired element for life." As the tears rolled down his cheeks, the princess in a tender gesture of love licked them off. The lovers were joined in profound emotion as they observed the magnificent sunset taking place. In a genuine gesture of reverence for nature's beautiful expressions in the midst of any circumstance, she savored her beloved's tears as if receiving nectar from the gods.

The prince, inspired by the sunset that had finally roused him from his bitter memories of the hard dryness he had to live through all his life, was deeply touched by the princess's ability to embrace with such warmth the only water he could provide her.

As sweet and tender as her gesture of acceptance seemed to him, the prince knew that she must continue to feel her own need for being provided by him of the most precious element in life. "Since she is lovingly savoring my tears," the prince thought, "she has to really like them, and so I really should provide her with more of them." Making now an effort, he continued to cry; to be sure she received enough tears. His wife on the other hand, did not like seeing him cry, not even in appreciation of nature's beauty and her feelings for him. She wanted to be a part of all his feelings and integrate in herself every emotion inhabiting his heart. It was in the core of her prince, in his inner most self that she wanted to exist.

Notwithstanding, it seemed to have been established, and the prince believed it was his duty, that he would be the provider of the liquid that his wife would most lovingly and with the greatest reverence incorporate into herself. He felt proud of his capacity of being the provider of fresh tears, and she felt her duty as a wife to continue to lick them off as fast as they rolled across his face, for this was her way of showing him that she was willing to participate in her husband's innermost feelings. They both enjoyed their participation in this loving ritual.

After a while of following their now established practice, in which she incorporated in herself the tears the prince would constantly provide, the meadow princess became thirsty, very thirsty, and nothing was enough to calm her thirst. The situation got to a point that she realized she had begun to dry up. The prince immediately understood that this was a matter of insufficient water, and that the only way to heal her condition would be to provide her with even more water than what she was already getting. At first, he made a sincere effort to provide her with as much tears as he possibly could so that she could go on drinking, but nothing he could manage to provide seemed to be enough. As soon as a tear came out of one of the prince's eyes, the princess would immediately lick it up, but she always ended up looking as forlornly dry as before. Finally, the day arrived when he realized he could not keep her moist because he was also drying up.

The meadow princess, coming from a land where there had always been plenty of water, was shocked to find herself drying up. Facing for the first time such a situation of extreme dryness and feeling acutely her own flow of life diminishing, in her desperation, she decided to seek out the only available water in vast amount that she knew how to reach—the ocean. She went to a nearby beach in order to reach the water's closest arriving point and once there she ran into the precious water to immerse herself in the liquid she so much needed. No one knew just how long she remained floating in the ocean's waters. She rejoiced at being in contact with this abundant resource of liquid she hadn't considered before, and was amazed to discover that the ocean's water tasted so similar to the flavor she had savored when drinking the tears of her beloved husband.

"There must be something sacred in my dear husband's precious tears and the ocean's waters that taste so very similar..." she thought to herself. After staying in the ocean for as long as she felt she needed, she came ashore and lay down on the sand under the bright warm sun hoping she had moistened herself enough to feel her usual softness. But

things did not turn out as she had expected. Instead of feeling relieved from her dryness, she now realized that her body was coated with white powder that made her skin feel tight and even dryer than before. Her body had absorbed so much salt that made her skin dry and itch all over.

By now, her mouth, her inner being and her skin, were longing and thirsty for fresh, sweet, unsalted water.

Moving with great difficulty because of her now-crusted body, she began walking home feeling very sad about her situation. Suddenly, she felt something fall on top of her head. "What would that be?" she wondered. "I hope it's nothing else I have to carry since I can already hardly move as it is and I don't know…" she did not finish the sentence for she realized that what she had felt were some drops of water. "What is this?" she wondered as she looked up into the sky and saw that it had begun raining. Very soon, the rain became heavy enough to leave her totally wet. "I am going to catch a cold!" she thought. "I feel weak and worn out, and now this rain…" But as she went on walking, even though the effort was great, contrary to her thoughts, she began feeling better. Her skin softened, and after a short while, she was comfortably moving, and walking as she was used to doing, and she was even jumping, as she once used to do in her home country. She instinctively opened her mouth to receive the water that continued to fall from the sky onto her very dry tongue, and soon she found herself actually drinking the heavenly water. After a while, she felt like dancing, and so she did, believing dancing in the rain is the way to be reborn. In the midst of this coming back so fully to herself, warm tears began rolling over her face and now she found herself savoring her very own source of water, something that in flavor combined the thick ocean's saltiness and the sweetness of the heavenly rain.

She arrived home soaked in water and joy. She changed into a soft satin dress and felt completely renewed, under the fabric her moistened flexible skin housing her soul, allowing every needed movement to take place. In this recovered state of being, she felt her tongue had been unstuck; its much needed moistness permitting her to speak more clearly than ever. She approached her beloved husband and said:

"My dear, I want to share with you some of the thoughts that have poured into my mind along with the many kinds of waters with which I have lately been in contact. I want you to know that I realize you have provided me with so much happiness since the very first moment we have been together. Because of that, I had forgotten everything else I even knew; I had even forgotten that I have in myself my own source of sacred water. As happy as I have felt living next to you, I would, every time I saw you crying, want to absorb whatever was making you unhappy. I had wanted to prove my love by sharing everything with you, and I thought that in my drinking your tears, I could relieve you of whatever had caused to sadden you. But I have seen how this only led to us both, you and me, to grow more and more dry. Your endless loving tears, and my endless loving drinking of them have really been drying us up. Today the heavenly waters were merciful enough to reveal this secret to me.

"I discovered that there is more than one god, more than one source of sacred water. I, who come from such a moist place, found out today that there are so many sources of dryness in life. But the one thing I learned I couldn't allow to take place, not even in the midst of the deepest devotion I feel towards our love, is failure to acknowledge and honor the deepest source of my own moist aliveness, the god I find inside myself. Blinded I had been to fail to see that my healing waters are contained in the depth of myself, and there can be no outside god to heal my dryness, my lacks, nor my sorrows. I truly love you, as I believe I will always do, but having you for my only god has resulted in drying up both of us. You, my provider of joy, of love, and life, were forgetting to provide for yourself too. You had lost touch with the precious moist I had discovered in you, which had the fragrance of the desert's blessings, and you, my found oasis, even have dried up when you tried to make yourself an endless provider for me."

Hearing these words, the prince immediately reacted:

"It is hard to accept what I am hearing from you. I have only tried to be the very best provider I could for you. Are you now saying that has been my mistake? Have I really heard you right? I know I have given you more than I actually had to give, but even though that is so, I have often thought that the dryness that came was my punishment for not being enough. I come from the desert—I spent years living there, and in all the days and nights I spent in that very dry land, I never felt so dry as I do now. While living in the desert, I saw and smelled the dryness I was surrounded with, in a never-changing landscape, except for when the wind arrived. And when that wind, even drier than the land because

it was filled with sand, attempted to cover everything, even myself, I learned how to protect my innermost moist. But here, in the midst of this green beautiful scenery, looking out on the extent of water that I can see every day, I have felt more entirely dry than ever in my life…"

As the prince heard himself talking, expressing the secret truth of his present dryness, which he had kept in silence all this time from the princess, he heard in the depths of his mind a question. "Could it be possible that the words she had spoken contained the truth that the sacred waters had always known? I left my land running away from dryness, only to find it here, once again, and now for some strange reason, her terrible words, which have hurt me so, feel refreshing."

Then he kept quiet. So did she. Time passed and the couple remained in their small oceanfront home. For her, dancing in the rain became a ritual, and she did it so often, particularly at sacred times, such as the beginning of spring or autumn, before getting pregnant and after delivering her babies. She was truly married, and with the changes this life brought, she seemed to need the moist of the heavenly waters outside herself to bring her in touch with her own inner endless and sacred source. As for him, he had the contrary need. On and off he went back to the desert where he grew up. He needed to see and touch its dryness, smell and feel his original land, and curiously it was by being in touch with its essential dryness that he was able to find and cherish his own moist.

Many years went by until these fortunate people had savored their truths enough to reach old age. One afternoon as they sat down to drink their usual tea, it was he who began by saying, "My dearest, it is time for me to thank you." "And what would that be for?" she asked. He had no trouble answering, "Many years ago, when you began dancing in the rain, and decided to get your moist replenished in that way, I felt totally pushed away from your life. Completely rejected, as I saw it then, I was so hurt and angry that I left for my own land, thinking that I would never be able to come back. But I got there and once again, in the midst of that desert land of my birth, living alone in nothingness, I was able to recover myself and discovered my moist all over again. And when I came back home, I found you soft and blooming. Of course I thought,

"Why should I stay here if she is complete without me? But as hurt as I was, I reflected that I too had newly regenerated moistness in myself, and it was really mine because you had no more need of it, not the way you had needed before when I thought that was why you loved me. Amazingly, in the midst of feeling I was no longer of use to you, I began to feel free, and able to feel the flow of my moist into a life I had never had before. This was my soul, and I need to say that I do not want to die without acknowledging what you enabled me to find."

Embracing with gratitude every word he had managed to finally say, the princess smiled. Her moist eyes and still-radiant skin seemed to beam a smile as well. As she kissed her husband's head, and in the softest, most liquid of voices, simply said, "Oh my forever love, may I serve you some tea?"

ONE OUTSIDE

Above the top of the highest mountains, posing over one of the most humid clouds, the Committee of Attributes gathered in their usual meeting in order to share their participation in the human lives. They were all present, as this meeting was accustomed to taking place every so often whenever the members who had formed this group sensed some lack of balance taking place on earth. The committee's main purpose was simply to take care of life in the order needed so that people on earth could lead their lives as whole as possible. For that purpose, maintaining a balance in the activities of the members of the committee was indispensable.

Attribute of Health arrived first, proud of himself as always because he knew his importance and the warm welcome he received among humans in the worst of situations. Following Health, of course was his partner, Sickness. This pair had much respect on earth, and they also respected each other when coming to know that at a certain point in human life, they were both needed.

Then, very shiny, as was his style of appearing, came Attribute of Success. He arrived as usual arguing with his partner, Attribute of Failure since both tended to impose their particular standing point. A bit later, in her characteristically mysterious smoky mode, Attribute of Beauty made her special entrance holding hands with her inevitable partner, Attribute of Ugliness. They were happy to come into the committee together, since they had found that keeping each other in view was the most efficient way for both to prove their true natures. Almost stepping on top of them came Attribute of Unfairness, leaving behind his partner, Attribute of Fairness. Not far behind was Attribute of Responsibility, running in place not to be late to the meeting and already making excuses for his partner, because Attribute of Irresponsibility was sure to be late as usual.

All the other attributes arrived together as pairs. Attribute of Discipline bringing his partner who usually forget the meetings. Attribute of Coldness and Attribute of Warmness strode in lockstep not even glancing at each other. Honesty and Dishonesty; Intelligence and Foolishness; Trust and Mistrust all followed suit, and when they sat down, they helped the rest to form a circle. When almost all of the attributes were seated and ready to begin their meeting, one more attribute arrived, all by herself. She was pale, weak, and skinny as if she had recently shrunk considerably. This was Attribute of Joy. She came in by herself and when asked about her partner, Absence of Joy, she responded, "He remained on earth."

Immediately, the other attributes wondered if that was the reason they were meeting today. Hearing the news that Absence of Joy was on earth, they began to look for the root causes in themselves. Attribute of Unfairness said, "I have been telling you, unfairness is spreading all over." "But how is that possible?" said Attribute of Responsibility. "We have an agreement," echoed Attribute of Commitment. "Yes," said Attribute of Duty, "we exist in pairs, and as difficult as it gets to have our balance, we know that by losing it, we endanger our very own existence."

"That Lack of Joy is on earth is terrible," said Attribute of Ugliness. "I can very well recognize how that could be the case." "I knew it would happen," agreed Attribute of Mistrust. "Nevertheless, they are right, we can't go on with this imbalance. We must intervene in what's happening on earth, because people have forgotten Attribute of Joy and that is dangerous," said Attribute of Intelligence. "How can one come close to be with humans? They don't even know how to be close to each other, so how do you imagine we are going to approach them?" commented Attribute of Coldness. "Well, perhaps they can approach us. It is not only us who need to help them—they also need us!" said Attribute of Foolishness. "Foolish as that sounds, I think he is right, but I'd put it the other way around. If we don't help the humans, we will be weakened as has already happened to Attribute of Joy," said Attribute of Sickness. He added, "If Attribute of Joy is not well, humans will also get sick..."

Then Attribute of Honesty spoke, "Let me be frank, my friends, I think we are the only ones who are aware of how much Attribute of Joy has ceased to matter on earth, and we are the ones who should be doing something to restore her presence there." Attribute of Success said, "That sounds right! We know how to do it. We know we can come down to earth with the rain of stars. We sure can do what's necessary." "But then what?" asked Attribute of Mistrust. "So we get there on our rain of stars. No one is expecting us to arrive, and as for Joy, perhaps humans have already forgotten what Joy is like!" "Us?" said Attribute of Beauty. "This is not about us. As much as I like to be seen, it is Attribute of Joy whose value has already vanished from the earth, who needs to reappear. I am sure if we can help her do this, her beauty will be recognized."

"What you say is true," said Attribute of Health, smiling at Beauty. "I have witnessed that as much as people are interested in being healthy, and do all sorts of things to preserve that wonderful asset, they are always delighted to experience Attribute of Joy!" Finally, Attribute of Joy spoke. "That was true, once. But now, I think, people are not interested anymore in Attribute of Joy. They are much too occupied with other things! And to be honest, I don't know how to make myself present to them anymore—their lives seem to have crowded me out…" Attribute of Trust then interrupted Joy, "You will find the way to do it. You can do so because you are the one who knows people are missing something that is terribly important in their lives. You are the joy of living, and they, every single human being, should not be missing what only you can bring into their lives."

"The rain of stars will soon begin," said Attribute of Commitment, who realized the time for deliberation was over. He addressed Joy saying, "Find your star, ride on her, you know your task! We will watch you from here, beaming our loyal support." "Each of us have also been forgotten at times. We can share your feelings, but you can't let yourself go on shrinking in its midst. It is already too dangerous that you have left the earth this long!" added Attribute of Warmth. At that precise moment, the rain of stars began. "Go, go now," exclaimed most of the attributes to Joy. "Go, go…" and off went Attribute of Joy, to find her particular mount from the beautiful rain of stars falling toward earth on that very night.

Late that same night, few people were up to watch this marvelous phenomenon, which rarely is seen on earth. But among the people who were willing to watch this rare appearance of stars in the sky was a man who really could not allow himself to go to bed. He was tired from a long day that had begun with a punishing early morning workout, followed by a non-stop routine of teaching at the university, managing his office staff, helping his wife with the household, and reading his one hundred and fifty pages a day, the goal he had set himself to live up to his title as Professor. Nevertheless, he was still awake at 2 AM waiting to see the unique rain of stars that had been announced to take place that night.

So deeply concentrating on the heavens was he that something fell on the top of his forehead, it felt so unimportant, so very light and subtle, that he did not pay any attention to what his senses had registered, that in fact a star had landed on him. When the visible rain of stars was over, he went to bed satisfied, even though he had only very few hours left in order to rest for the new working day that was soon to begin.

When morning arrived, the man jumped out of bed in order to begin his new perfectly ordered day. As he did every morning, he put on his sweat pants, sunscreen lotion, and special shoes for his tired feet, his cap, and pocketed his smart phone, in case someone should need anything from him before he actually started working. When he was ready to leave his house, checking to make sure he had his keys, he found his dog welcoming his master, totally alert and strongly wagging his tail to signal, he too, was ready to take their morning walk.

But this morning, the man saw the very well-known sequence of actions when his dog began barking and jumping, eagerly waiting for the door to open, only on that particular day something about his dog's enthusiasm caused the professor to ask himself, "How do I celebrate our morning walk? My encounter with the first beams of light, with the fresh air, he makes it clear how he considers it a privilege to walk out of the house with me for our morning walk. He is totally into his embodied celebration of a new day that we can share. But what about me?" Do I ever celebrate anything at all?" Such were the thoughts of the professor, who after all was a philosopher. And immediately, he came up with an answer that reflected his commitment to his schedule. "Oh for goodness sake, I am only losing time thinking nonsense. What has gotten into my head this morning?" And that question he found easy to answer, "It must be because I went so very late to bed and broke my schedule that I am in such a mood this morning." With that, he left with his happy dog to fulfill the morning exercise plan and once done went back home to take his shower, afraid that he was going to be late for work.

But in the shower, fresh unusual thoughts descended upon him. He suddenly discovered, as if this was the very first bath he had ever taken, how pleasant it was experiencing the water running over his skin, "What a nice feeling," he said aloud to himself and immediately he began to explain it away. "It must be that I just managed to turn the faucet to get the right water temperature that has delighted my skin," he reflected silently. Then his thought process added, "They have just cleaned the water pipes, and that's why the water looks so crystalline this morning… perhaps I was too sweaty and that is why the water feels so very fresh…" After getting that far in explaining a feeling he had never in fact felt before on his always tired and tensed body, a harsh voice spoke from within, "What is the matter with you today, to make you dawdle with silly questions and useless answers?" The professor lowered his head and said to himself, "Yes, I am only losing time, I should have been already dressed by now, and gone to work! I will really be late!"

He left his house, walking faster, and was thankful when he arrived at the University on time. There, he continued his usual busy day, drawing upon the attributes of Discipline, Responsibility, and Commitment that commanded him—driven by a constant sense of Duty that had to be fulfilled. Performance, efficiency, and achievement were what he taught his students to strive for, as he himself went on with his non-stop ritual.

But even so, as he followed his already set agenda, he could not ignore the fact that some strange sparkles of unfamiliar pleasure that accompanied his thoughts and feelings kept appearing, making his impeccable behavior seem a bit less perfect. Strangely, he did not exactly dislike what had begun to happen, but he was unable to recognize that something had begun to accompany his usual approach to life. He finally baptized the interfering sparkles of delight that had been born that morning as *inadmissible nonsense.*

Later that same week, after a cold rainy day, he arrived home glad to have the bowl of hot soup that his wife had prepared for him. It felt so satisfying to his empty stomach and so nourishing to his tired body, that he wondered how something entirely so simple could give him such a total feeling of wellbeing. "Or is it me?" He wondered, but almost immediately, he replied to himself, "That must be because I didn't have time to eat lunch earlier today." And then he was quite firm about not going further with self-reflection. "Enough!" he said, almost aloud. "I have had it with this *nonsense* that would like to go on interrupting my life, day after day. Now, before I have to go to bed, it is time to read my daily one hundred and fifty pages, otherwise, I will not be updated with everything that is being published these days."

With that, he began to read, but the need to follow his precise routine wore him out. Rather quickly, he fell asleep on the cozy sofa in his studio, where his dog soon joined him. He slept all the way though until the next morning.

When he woke up to the full shining sun coming through the window, he realized he had not heard the alarm clock, because he was not in his bed. He felt so well rested, as he had not felt in years, that he stretched his body with pleasure, and it was only then that he became aware that it was really late. "Oh my God! How could this happen? I just fell asleep and now what? It is so late, what a shame! This is unacceptable!" And as he spoke to himself, he left running to work.

Nobody else said anything. During that day, he suddenly found himself as if in reverie wondering about what was going on inside him. Perhaps the disturbance in his schedule wasn't that important to anyone else, but that wasn't the point. He did not have an answer for why it had happened. All he knew was that it was disturbing and shameful and he was beginning to lose efficiency, punctuality, and accuracy, and could no longer maintain his carefully established order. For that to be altered from now on would be unforgivable.

Nevertheless, he continued to be annoyed by the sparks of *inadmissible nonsense* that kept happening practically every day. As time passed, though hard to accept, he was immersed in shame when he finally recognized that he was almost looking forward to these interruptions. Horrified by his feelings, he became even more severe in his discipline and resolves to stand by his rigidly established life. The tension got to be so very powerful between the insistent seductiveness of the *inadmissible nonsense* that kept appearing and his devotion to his well-structured life that the day arrived when he knew he simply couldn't go on with this situation anymore. He decided to take some time away from his work, his home, his family, and his very few friends. It would only be for a very few days, he reasoned, but he needed time to be with himself.

"Why are *you* leaving?" was the frequent question he was confronted with by the people surrounding him. "I feel too tired, so I think I need some time off," was the only answer they were given. Even the professor could not imagine any other reason for taking time away other than the impossibility of continuing with the way his life had been in the recent weeks. All he knew was, he was hoping to put an end to the nonsense and return to the usual order of his life. With that thought, he took off for parts unknown.

As he did so, Attribute of Joy, who had been watching him, confirmed her decision that she would not engage in talking directly with this man, since it was very clear to her that Joy is something for him to experience and not just hear about. So it happened that without really deciding where he would go for his time off, the man arrived at a small hotel where he decided on the spot to spend some days. Attribute of Joy felt that was perfect. She now had a stage on which to show him the importance of her very own nature. The man unknowingly, had, opened himself to experiencing something that until then had never been allowed to exist within his life. He spent some sensuous days in which he could feel the pleasure of being immersed in warm, soapy water. He took luxurious long baths in no hurry at all; he felt the sun caressing his face when he went outside; he took long walks that enabled him to discover the rhythm of his breathing, and he loved to hear his heart pounding when he did so. The food he ate appeared to be delicious, and sleeping was so very restoring that it was hard to believe how well he felt. So overwhelmed was he with these simple delights, which were entirely new to him that for the first time in his life he did not think much.

Sooner than he wanted, the day arrived when he had to return home and get back to work. Far from what his initial plan had predicted, being able to put an end to the *inadmissible nonsense*, on the day he was leaving this special place, he found himself thinking, "Oh, I am going to miss this…this. I know I have to return, but…can it be possible? I am feeling sad that I have to leave this special place."

As he was driving home, he continued to feel sad. Not knowing why this feeling stayed with him, he scolded himself. "That is all I needed now!" He immediately began thinking about all the things he had to do, and about the many responsibilities he had left unattended the last few days. Before he arrived home, his mind was already full with all the duties that had piled up to fulfill.

The next morning, he got up even earlier than usual. He immediately dived into the commitments he had abandoned. He toiled that day with a very great sense of responsibility, for he now had to make up for all the lost times. In this state of mind, he went on working intensely for several days more.

As time passed by, it was the man who was losing weight and looking pale. But his mind was not entirely on his work. He kept thinking of going back to that small hotel which had offered him something he did not want to forget and could hardly believe existed. With great difficulty, he decided finally that he had to go back once again, though for less days than before. When he arrived at the special hotel, far from the duties that were still clamoring to be fulfilled, he was able to admit to himself how much he needed this place of solitude, even though it made him feel guilty. It was here, away from his usual agenda, that he could allow himself to actually experience the nonsense that kept appearing. Back in this unique and longed for place, he could embrace what had so much been missing in his life. He could not identify the emotion that arose then, and he certainly could not name it, but as the hours went by, he began thinking how much he also liked his dutiful life. He started to actually miss being at the university, miss the experience of going to his office, and of returning to his home and the people he loved. And so, he went back to his established life.

The professor could scarcely endure having such opposite emotions. Going back and forth in his mind between the relief he could now experience when he could allow himself to get away from work, and the homesickness for work he knew he would feel when he went away was exhausting! He was not used to a life that was so incomprehensible.

Attribute of Joy, aware of what she had caused by the way she now introduced herself into his life, realized that she needed to share with her fellow Attributes what was taking place on earth. Joy went back with the wind to the top of the mountain. Light as she had become, it only took some brief moments for her to arrive in time to attend the Committee of Attributes, which was once again gathering. As she was among her fellows, she began talking even before saying hello. "I had wanted him to be joyful. That is what I really wanted. I had wanted to be included in his life! But I had forgotten to consider what it is like for humans to feel joy! More often than not, it felt to me like he was afraid of enjoying, and I can see now that he does not dare to enjoy his life! I wonder how can that be possible, but it is true!" Every other Attribute listening to Joy's recent experience on earth, kept quiet. They realized she had an urge in sharing her experience, and so they allowed Joy to go on talking. "I have been so very afraid of being left out and vanishing all together, that I wanted him to be all joy. I have been so pushed away that I thought the only possible way of existing was in the absolute mode, thus taking over what I consider a miserable life made out of duties to be fulfilled one after the other."

Listening to Joy's confession, Attribute of Beauty, who until then had been quiet, suddenly interrupted saying, "In my experience among humans I have visited, there are those who really do lead horribly duty-burdened lives! Probably this man is one of them. When I encounter a life like that, I think to myself, why should I try to stay here? People who are bent on making themselves miserable certainly can't recognize me! And I don't want to be around them! And even when I am also aware that our existence depended on humans, I prefer to be among people who can embrace me, and I have found that some of them can even adore me! Those are the ones to whom I can prove life's extensive beauty. So tell me Joy, why are you so insistent about putting yourself in this man's life?"

Joy was struck by Attribute of Beauty's question, so she took some time to think and after a while, she said, "I believe I have insisted on making myself present to him because I have long been noticing how joy has fallen into disregard among humans. Joy has become such an irrelevant aspect of life for them, so much in miss-use that I have grown afraid that people will soon forget the existence of Joy. Their lives are so very busy and crowded that they just don't have time for joy. When I go down to earth, I see humans in their rush of life not even looking for me. That is why I took the space and time with this man who still had the time and willingness to look into the sky and watch the rain of stars, to hopefully recover his loss of joy. But what I have ended up witnessing, and why I am coming to all of you now, is that my fellow attributes, Responsibility, Commitment, and Discipline, have taken up all the space in the man's life! And contrary to what I thought, I ended up realizing that their existence is indeed not only important, but very much needed for this man who cannot be joyful in abandoning all of you, dear attributes, who are also part of his life."

The other attributes were about to interrupt when Joy continued, "But I recognize that I have been blinded by my fear of not having a place in the human realm. That made me try too hard to call attention to myself. I know, and I want to tell all of you, that Joy will only earn a real lasting space when I accept that I am part of a much more complex and rich array of attributes. I was not born to live a separate life because staying as an outsider also puts me at risk. "So…" concluded Joy, in a speech that was like music to the ears of her fellow attributes, "I am beginning to think that perhaps my task is different than what I had thought—it is not just a matter of my making life joyful. My job is to include myself in already built up lives that have many other aspects. You see, I have not done this man a favor by creating such deep longing for joy that he has to feel guilty for abandoning all the other attributes that are already present in his life. Do you understand?" asked Joy. "The only way for him to experience joy was outside his very own life!"

Joy probably would have said even more when Attribute of Foolishness interrupted what seemed to him to be too long a discourse already. "Excuse me for interrupting, but I am not understanding what you are talking about, and even worse, I can't recognize you any longer when you share all this worrying with us. Who are you now Joy? What has happened to you? Where are you Joy? Did you leave that on earth?" As usual, he pleaded failure to understand what he just heard.

It was then that Attribute of Intelligence realized it was his turn to speak, for only he could clear up Foolishness' confusion. "It seems to me that there are two things going on simultaneously. On one hand, a man on earth has fallen into being a prey of joyful enchantment, and so feels the need for a whole new life, a life outside the one that has been his own up to now in order to start living in pure joy. It is as if he would now be an attribute himself! On the other hand, and this is even more weird, you, Joy, who really is an attribute, sound like you have been humanized! But that is not a process that corresponds to you. You are an attribute, and an attribute only, you have no body, you can't live on earth, and as much as you can and want to share with your fellow attributes, you cannot incorporate us in yourself and take over the human roll. We cannot allow that to happen, because if you do that, how then is the human to experience joy? You have to remember, as we all do, that it is for us attributes to faithfully and purely remain for what we are—and nothing else."

"Humans," said Attribute of Intelligence, "have the privilege of existing only for a limited time. They are mortals, and for that little time they remain on earth, they have a *cuerpo* in which they have the chance to *in-corpore* (incorporate) us into their lives. It is because of their living bodies that human beings have the container, the vessel in which all type of combinations and reactions can take place; their bodies are their labs where they mix and match, play and create while they are living on earth, and it is through what happens in those labs that they can become real human beings, in the very essence of what that means, but it is in them where creation takes place. We attributes, are quite different, we don't require bodies. We have the singularity in our natures of being only what we are built for. We are the elements, and we exist forever in our purity. We must remain who we are for humans to be able to fulfill their task of incorporating, balancing, and re-creating what we can offer to their chemistry, again and again, during their lifetime. As attributes, we live through them, but we cannot turn any human being into a sole attribute in order to grant one of us existence, otherwise, an attempt to live different lives in one sole body takes place and that is impossible. We have to content ourselves with sharing the very same body. Humans cannot be *us*—they are granted the possibility of including, experiencing, changing, and dancing with, among all of us. But they are not *us*—they should not be. They are humans."

When hearing these words, Attribute of Unfairness raised himself and voiced his own position in this argument. "Listen, this traditional thinking is totally unfair to Joy. Joy went to earth and she has learned something new that she brought to share with all of us here, and even though she is here, we cannot even hear her. It's silly to tell her to forget about being human—we all know this is not what we are. What we need to do is hear what Joy has to say. We have to remember she has become an endangered attribute!"

After this intervention, Joy went on, once again, with what she so much wanted to say, but it was difficult to formulate: "This will sound strange to you, for it does even to me, but I think I could even begin by expressing appreciation for one of you from whom I have always wanted to keep myself totally apart, Lack of Joy." Hearing these words, everybody shared a bewildered silence. This was broken by Attribute of Foolishness, who said, "I have already told you, this is incomprehensible. What is she talking about now?" But then, Attribute of Trust, who had already sensed the need of her intervention said, "Let's hear her out, it will be fine, let's just see what she has been able to discover during her most recent visit to Earth."

With this support, Joy felt able to continue. "The night I left in order to go to earth was a very dark one. Not even the moon was shining. I clung close to the star I was riding in the beautiful rain of stars. As I was riding down to earth, I saw the very darkness of the sky, and I noticed in that deeply obscure blackness that there were unmistakable momentary sparks of light. The twinkling stars in the firmament shined at its fullest, illuminating not only the star I was embracing, but also the stars raining down around her. And not just them, when the stars of the firmament twinkled, even the darkest of earth skies got to be lightened. Following that brief moment of illumination was when the star I was riding, and the sky, lost brilliance all over again. No one looking at us from earth would believe there was any star in the sky. It was only because I was holding so tight to the one star transporting me that I happen to know they exist. I could feel between my own imaginary wings that even when a star does not visibly shine forth, and no one believes in its existence, that star remains in force. And if it is one's own star, one must not abandon it just because one cannot momentarily see it. One has to hold tight trusting that after a while, its shine will appear once again. For me, in my lack of belief that in such darkness, any light would ever reappear, it was a revelation when the magnificent and much awaited light of my own star arrived. And I have to say, this happened again and again during my ride to earth in which each blaze of the light I was embracing was always followed by another dark moment. This was what took place during my long trip to earth, which gave me time to experience how it was the darkness that gave such meaning to the shining light of my star." Joy took a deep breath and then continued, "When I had realized that, it occurred to me that it is Lack of Joy that must accompany me. Finally, I learned that I must hold tight to myself, to my own nature, just as I did with the star I was riding. I am Joy, and even in the darkest of times when feeling the threat of nonexistence, I know from experience that light can appear once again, and so can Joy.

After hearing Joy out, the Committee of Attributes began to murmur among themselves what a relief it was to all of them that Joy had recovered herself. They saw how important she was for the people living on earth. Her willingness to go on being herself even in dark times meant that people, in their attempts to become truly human, would not have to go outside their very own and already built up lives to find a very weak and endangered Attribute of Joy thus needing total devotion to herself. Instead she would always be around as her authentic, joyful self.

When this conversation took place on the very top of the mountain where the attributes gather, Joy was able to recover her confidence, and strange as it was, that had an effect on the professor Joy had visited on earth. Very gradually, he learned that in the midst of hard work, discipline, responsibility, and punctuality, the virtues which formed the very structure that he sustained for the rest of his life, he nevertheless, was able to find his very own way to "wag his tail" and celebrate his actual home, work, people and life.

What had once taken place in that little hotel to which he would, from time to time still visit, remained a mystery. It was in that small place where he encountered some very new things, far from what the university, his office, and his constant readings taught him, in that secluded space, where he only had himself to take care of, that he experienced depth, inspiration and wholeness. And what he once used to call *inadmissible nonsense*, which now and then would appear in his very own mind, keeping their marvelous, mysterious and threatening nature, he now calls *sparkles of Joy* with the deepest sense of committed contentment.

UAYAMON

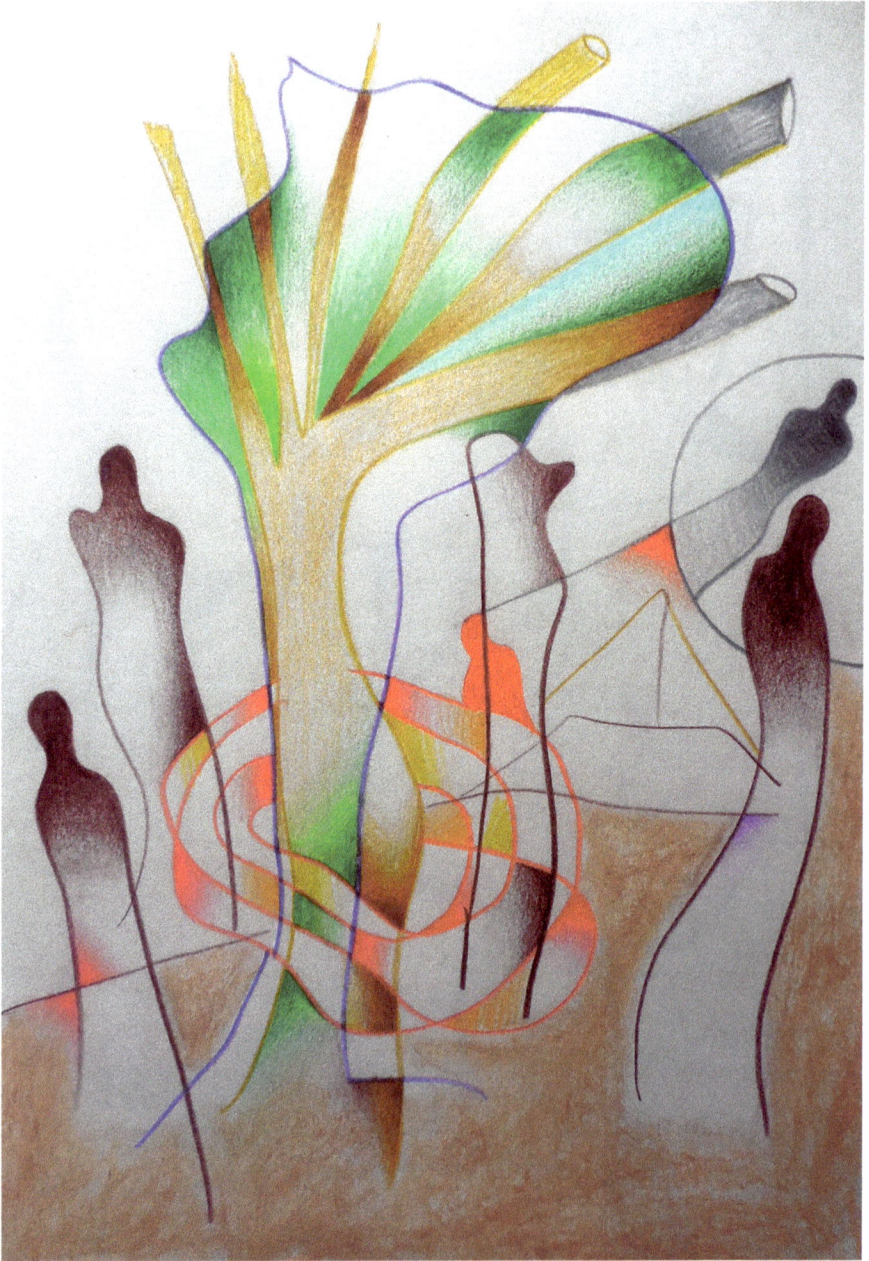

There, around the ancient *Ceiba*, sacred tree of the Mayas, the spirits came down dancing. One midnight, after a silvery evening that had been warm and humid, as the moon was crossing the sky it was caught by the sight of the *Ceiba*, the magnificent tree of life. The moon paused for a brief moment. The huge *Ceiba*, honorably standing in its enormous proportions, was illuminated. The land was still, and everything at the *Hacienda* was asleep, resting in the quiet the night offered after such an intense sunny day. And it was then that the spirits came out to dance around the *Ceiba* in order to fulfill their functions for the community.

The moon witnessed that the spirits had chosen this time to infuse their vital force so that life could continue. Just how they did this was of course a mystery. It had something to do with what happened when they danced around the tree, because that dance had to be just right, and continuous. The moon reflected its light on the spirits with enormous admiration. But there was one, a small nutty spirit that kept turning and twirling around and around, and for some unknown reason, did not keep step with the rest of his fellow spirits. Night was over, finally the first rays of sun appeared and human motion began again, its energy source had been renewed. Facing the brightness of the sun, the moon was ready to hide her face when, to her surprise, she heard a spirit voice saying, "Take me with you! Take me with you! Tonight I seem to be too heavy to lift myself. My peers have left, because I could not keep up with them, but I cannot be seen on earth, this is neither the time nor the place for a spirit to be visible. I must be lost, so take me with you, and help me hide myself away." The moon, who had already turned her face and was ready to present herself to the other side of earth, which was just entering darkness, was astonished to hear this spirit speak. None of them ever did. As confusing as the phenomenon was, she could not allow it to stop her from carrying out her duties. She answered honestly, "I'm sorry, I cannot take you with me, for I would get lost myself if I did. I can't even stay to talk to you. I must leave now because the other side of earth is waiting for me." And then, as if reflecting just a bit more before having to depart, she told the lost spirit, "I have been doing my rounds for endless of time, I can show you where you can hide, but you will have to wait where I tell you, for an entire cycle until I am full again. Only then will you be able to join your fellow spirits. In the meantime,

I will come visit you every night, where you are hiding and you may tell me about yourself and how you experience remaining on earth." "I will do what you say," the spirit replied.

While this unusual conversation was taking place, the sun, threatening with his shine, got to be closer and closer. "I can see we have to be quick," said the spirit to the moon, "so guide me at once to the place you mentioned, I will follow the gleam of your light, it is impossible to stay here, it is too dangerous, and much too light. I have felt the sun coming, I must not be here." The moon sent one of her clearest cool beams, pointing toward the safest place for the spirit to hide. Taking only one breath for air, the spirit arrived to where he knew to remain for all of the moon cycle.

The moon had left. The sun was brightly shining. The *Hacienda* was awake. The spirit, whose name was Confusion, was for the first time in his life, happy not to be seen.

He was aware, however, of carrying a heavy weight, which did not belong to him. Nevertheless, he remained hidden without moving or making any sound. No one at all was able to see him. That was his day.

When it became dark, as it happens every night, the moon appeared in the sky, as punctual as she had been since the beginning of time. But this time, she was keeping a promise. Right at midnight, she arrived to visit the spirit of confusion, just as she had said she would do. "Are you there?" she asked, to which Confusion immediately answered. "Yes, of course I am. I have been waiting for you. It is good to see you. In fact, I wanted to ask you, since our conversation last night turned out to be so fast. Just where is it that I am hidden?"

The moon's answer was surprising. "This is the hospital that was built for the *Hacienda*."

"What is a hospital?" asked the spirit.

"Somewhere people go in order to be healed," answered the moon.

"Do they really believe they need this place for healing to take place?" said the spirit.

"It appears so," answered the moon. "They come here when something aches, or when they are in even greater suffering."

"But why would they come here?" asked the spirit. "Have they forgotten us? Forgotten the spirits, forgotten that we dance around the *Ceiba*?"

"That's a good question," replied the moon. "One I am not sure I can answer. All I really know is what I see, and have seen that this is the place where they come when pain takes over their lives, and they can't go on enjoying. Would you like to know the specific name they have given to the hospital?"

"Yes I would, what is it?" said the spirit of confusion.

"Hospital of Mercy," said the moon.

Confusion was more confused than ever. "Mercy? Is that what they are lacking? Is that what they come here for? How could that possibly be missing? What do you think happened, Milady Moon?"

Moon stayed quiet for a while and then she said, "I will answer only if you also let me ask you a question, does that sound fair? I should say it would be a personal one."

"I will certainly try to answer, please go ahead," responded the spirit.

The moon went ahead saying, "First, I will try answering your question. I will try doing so because I have felt myself the suffering in the people who arrive at the hospital, their state of emergency and fear, and the ache of deep pain, which they seldom admit to. So I have personally sensed in them a very great lack, a desperate need for something, and I have realized that they themselves don't know what it is. They have to get all type of sickness to come here for what has been missing all along. Perhaps the name they came up with for the hospital is exactly what they are lacking, Mercy. I hope that answers your question. But if you are still confused, it could be because my way of answering a question is never so precise as to stop further questions from coming. And in fact that leads me to the question I want to ask you. How can you, the very spirit of confusion, be so very clear when you talk? You are clear in asking, are you as clear in observing? You confuse me, because you don't seem to be confused at all!"

"You are right Milady Moon," said Confusion, with a touch of sadness in his voice. "My greatest confusion is that I am so very clear about what I don't understand. Hardly anyone I've ever met is like me..." But he could not finish this answer, because by then the moon had moved on in her nightly round, caressing every surface of the earth with her subtle, silvery gloom.

The next day, Confusion went around the hospital, trying to answer his own question. He certainly heard the people complain about their aches. He believed them when they said they were suffering. Now no one saw him, since he was a spirit, but the energy of his confused compassion started to permeate through the pores of the walls of this place where people had come in hopes that their suffering could at least be understood and contained. When the night arrived, the moon came back, this time looking a bit thinner, as if she had reduced her brightness on her long journey around the world.

"Are you feeling okay?" asked the spirit. His concern was over how she had diminished in size, but the moon reassured him. "I am really perfectly fine," replied the moon. "You simply have not seen me smaller since you have only visited the earth before when you came to dance, and those were times when I was big and fully shining, and then I light up your dance. Now I am waning, this is my cycle, I have been on it since the beginning of time."

"It is so helpful to me that you tell me this," said the spirit. "I have wondered why the night gets to be darker and cooler after you come— why it doesn't simply heat up and stay that way after one of your brilliant visits that always gave me and my fellow spirits the energy to dance." But again, without even taking her leave of this promising conversation, the moon had moved on and the spirit was in the very darkness of the night.

Days, and nights like this passed in sequence, and the spirit of confusion went around the hospital adding what he could to its mercy. He was cheered by the moon that kept arriving every night, even though at this point in her cycle, she was becoming smaller and smaller. The one bad thing was, as she grew tinier, she stayed less time, and conversation became even harder to sustain. Finally, the night arrived when the moon did not show up at all, nor did he hear even a sliver of her voice. It was deeply dark, and the people at the Hospital of Mercy, who had grown used to sensing the confused spirit's kind energy, could not feel

his presence at all. They themselves became confused. So deep was the confusion, that people began doubting even the reality of their own symptoms, despite the fact that they continued to suffer from them. Doubting their own pain, they also doubted their reason to have arrived at the Hospital of Mercy. They certainly felt utterly confused as to where they would find any true healing for a condition they were not even sure was legitimate. In this way, even though he never actually saw or felt their worry, the spirit of confusion was clearly present. The full effect of his own confusion was felt. It had permeated everyone at the hospital as to why they were at the *Hacienda*. For the first time, the healers were confused about their task and participation, and what healing they could provide at the *Hacienda*, which to them was no longer a hospital. Like the patients, the healers were no longer clear as to what they were really trying to heal. Their previous certainty about what was best for each of the people asking for help had vanished.

Recognizing their confusion, the Caretaking Healers decided it was best to slow down on the dispensing of therapeutic rituals and even hold off from deciding, as they were used to doing each morning, as to the best treatment to be offered for each patient in the hospital. They knew they had to observe themselves and try to figure out what was taking place in their own systems to have brought them to this point of therapeutic confusion. To that, they had to forego seeing their patients until they had taken, for the first time, a deep hard look at themselves as they were being confronted with their own confusion.

Under these circumstances, the patients in the hospital were forced to take a much more active role in the healing process they were expecting. These people had arrived at the Hospital of Mercy asking for help, but now they began wondering if they really wanted help. They had first to answer whether they even wanted to go on living the lives they had been asking others to save. Now they asked themselves, why would we want to live the very same life we are used to living, given the state of pain we are in? Do we really want to keep the very same life that brought us to be in the miserable condition that brought us to this Hospital of Mercy? Their confusion was deeper than ever.

In the meantime, people living and working at the *Hacienda* were themselves confused about what had been happening at the Hospital of Mercy. These ordinary caretakers had been locked out of the rituals of healing for such a long period of time that it no longer occurred to them to wonder if the patients were getting what they needed. But now, when there was no movement in the hospital corridors, when no one went in or out of the rooms reserved for healing, the hospital seemed to be much too still. The *Hacienda* staff realized something must have happened. Certainly no patient had left to return to his or her usual life for a very long time. Outside the Hospital of Mercy, stories began piling up regarding the healing activities that must have been taking place to keep the people detained at the hospital. But few found these stories reassuring.

Still some of what was being ventured as an explanation was interesting. Among the tales that were passed around, there was the one about the illness of a woman who did not make a wise use of her energy and so got punished. Her punishment consisted in the fact that every time a man wanted to come near her, spines would grow out of her body such that no one would be able to embrace her. "That can take a lot of time to heal," said a few people in the community who added, "She certainly needs help at the Hospital of Mercy for such a dreadful situation. She will need a longer than usual stay."

There was also the story of the wax dog—a dog made of wax, which would come alive when fed with the blood of men. They wanted to prove the power of their blood to bring to life a wax dog. But they were shocked when the dog finally became alive and turned out to be a ferocious beast that without hesitation began biting those very same men whose blood had fed him into being. "Those men must also be asking for help, we have seen some men like this in our community— seeking to be healed from being beaten up by a wax dog whose bite was their own creation!"

And then, there was the couple, whose hearts were eternally aching because they couldn't come close enough to each other. Both of them carried such a heavy load of pain in their bodies that it blocked any possible movement that would be required to get near each other. "How then were they able to arrive at the Hospital of Mercy?" wondered some of the younger members of the community, who hadn't yet learned not to ask such questions when a story was being told. "It must have been out of deep love and compassion that they roused themselves from their individual pains to come together to our hospital," they told themselves. "Well, they had to do so if they wanted to heal their bodies and their souls that hurt so terribly," responded a young woman who was impatient with her fellows for raising this question.

In short, all kinds of tales were being told at the *Hacienda* while the Hospital of Mercy remained under its spell of confusion. Finally one night, a beam of light appeared. The moon was beginning to shine in the dark sky once again. The spirit of confusion welcomed her warmly. "You are back! It is so good to see you. We are in need for some of your light." "I can see that, for you are still here!" said the moon to the spirit of confusion.

"All right then, I will help. Tonight, I can only say hello, but from today on, I will be coming back every night bringing more light and we can spend some bright nights together. It will not be only tonight that I return. I promise I will be back soon," and saying this, the moon and her light vanished into the depth of the sky.

As promised, from that day on, the moon came back every night. When she had grown bright enough to have space and time for a real conversation with the spirit of confusion, she went on manifesting her curiosity regarding the question he hadn't answered. "So, if you remember," said the moon, "you were going to answer my question of how can you, the very spirit of confusion, be so entirely clear?"

So he answered, "First of all, you are right Milady Moon, I am clear. But I can be clear only because I have been so very confused. Let me remind you that confusion is the step before clarity. You know that there was a time before even you existed, a time before day and night had come into being, and surely at that time there was already confusion. Everything was a huge, great confusion. It was out of this confusion that your own life began, because you were the light in the night! That is often forgotten. But I have not forgotten it. The confusing darkness is what brought me into being.

"From time to time," continued the spirit of confusion, "I am requested on earth—for some reason I become important among humans. Fortunately for me, though, there are those like you who have finally been able to come out of the confusion, to show all of us the way to clarity. And believe me, I am not necessarily a good spirit or a protector of life, nor am I an evil spirit driving people into scary and desperate confusion. I am Confusion, this is my nature and you are the light that comes in the night that makes confusing things clear."

"But that is not quite enough," said the moon. "How do you choose when or where to appear? What gave you that ability to choose?"

"But I don't get to choose!" said the spirit of confusion. "All I know is that when I become heavy, then I must remain on earth. There, I do my job, which is getting other people to share my nature. When I feel lighter once again, which is usually by the time you are full and bright, I can leave the world to its confusion and I go back with my fellow spirits."

This conversation went on, while the moon kept moving across the sky. Finally she had to interrupt. "I will be back tomorrow."

The next morning was a humid and warm day. People who had stayed inside the Hospital of Mercy finally began to come out. Nothing was said by them, nor asked of them. Life at the *Hacienda* seemed to go on without anyone really knowing what had happened to the population of the Hospital of Mercy. But for those who had remained there, they were aware of the feeling, that in the midst of great confusion and their long aching souls, a new light had kindled. A healing light which had taken residence in each of them, as they came out of their long-enough stay at the Hospital of Mercy.

Night arrived to find people at the *Hacienda* peacefully resting, and the moon once again chatting, just as she had promised, with the spirit of confusion.

"Good evening, Confusion," said the moon, in her calm but definite voice. "May I ask about your work? I see people leaving the hospital, how are they feeling? What follows now?" It was obvious she had been witnessing the change in the population of the hospital. The spirit of confusion, honest as always, answered, "I don't know what follows." "What do you mean you don't know?" asked the moon. "It was you who created this confusion!" To which the spirit added, "Yes, that was my task, but that is done, and it is not for me to know what follows. Am I being clear?" asked the spirit, turning to the moon for her superior clarity. "I remained on earth because I suddenly felt myself too heavy to

rise and leave with my fellow spirit friends, and I had to remain where that extra weight held me down. In that way, I was able to stop carrying things that do not belong to me. By unloading that weight at last, I have been completing my own task, which was always to create confusion, not to carry it for others. If I don't complete my task, I can't keep up with other spirits, and I cannot rejoin and do my very own dance.

"But let me share with you Milady Moon what I found out during my stay at the Hospital of Mercy. People there were also loaded with weight—not their own—that was not allowing them to go on dancing their lives. My job was to bring what I am and make them confused so that they now have to start sorting out how little weight belongs to each of them if they ever want to dance again in their lives. I participated in unburdening them, as we spirits often do, infusing movement and vitality in people who had been weighed down too long. That is what a spirit does, and confusing or not, I am no exception. Now that I have done my task," said the spirit of confusion, "I would like to ask you if you would be so kind as to guide me with your light to the *Ceiba*, where my fellow spirit friends will be dancing tonight once again. I want to rejoin them, and I know they will be glad to welcome me back."

Nothing else was heard. The moon kept quiet, respectfully understanding what had been said. She did as she was asked and guided the spirit of confusion to the tall and honorable standing tree, the *Ceiba*, where other spirits had already descended to do their dance. They welcomed the spirit of confusion, whom, thanks to the light of the moon, they could see had returned to be with them once more. Together, with his fellow friends whose descent he had joined, all of them, once again as they have done for centuries, took pleasure in their eternal spiritual dance. They did so tonight under the brightest possible light of a beautiful full moon.

UAYAMON: "Mayan word meaning: "Where the spirits descend."

BIOGRAPHICAL NOTES

Jacqueline Gerson is a Jungian analyst with a private practice in Mexico City, where she works as an analyst, teacher, and supervisor. With a lifelong passion for dance and movement, she first approached dreams as spontaneous choreographies created by the psyche. Eventually, that discovery led her to the study of Analytical Psychology to become an individual member of the IAAP. She lectures on topics related to analytical psychology and has been published in *The San Francisco Jung Institute Library Journal*, with Daimon Verlag, Brunner-Routledge, *Spring Journal*, as well as the Mexican magazine *Epoca*. As a new way for her to relate to most sensitive aspects in life, writing stories became apparent. Her special joys are grandmothering, dance movement, writing, poetry, and nature.

Saúl Kaminer was born in Mexico City on July 8, 1952. He graduated as an architect from the Mexican National University (UNAM). He started his artistic work in 1970 and moved to Paris in 1976 where he worked intensely in his paintings and sculptures. After 22 years in France, Saul continued his artistic work in Mexico. So far, he has had 65 individual expositions and participated in 160 collective expositions in various countries in the Americas, Europe, and Asia.

You might also enjoy reading:

Marked By Fire: Stories of the Jungian Way edited by Patricia Damery &
Naomi Ruth Lowinsky, 1st Ed., Trade Paperback, 180pp, Biblio., 2012
— ISBN 978-1-926715-68-1

The Dream and Its Amplification edited by Erel Shalit & Nancy Swift
Furlotti, 1st Ed., Trade Paperback, 180pp, Biblio., 2013
— ISBN 978-1-926715-89-6

Shared Realities: Participation Mystique and Beyond edited by Mark
Winborn, 1st Ed., Trade Paperback, 270pp, Index, Biblio., 2014
— ISBN 978-1-77169-009-6

Pierre Teilhard de Chardin and C.G. Jung: Side by Side edited by Fred
Gustafson, 1st Ed., Trade Paperback, 270pp, Index, Biblio., 2014
— ISBN 978-1-77169-014-0

Jungian Child Analysis edited by Audrey Punnett, 1st Ed., Trade Paperback,
240pp, Index, Biblio., 2018
— ISBN 978-1-77169-038-6

Re-Imagining Mary: A Journey Through Art to the Feminine Self
by Mariann Burke, 1st Ed., Trade Paperback, 180pp, Index, Biblio., 2009
— ISBN 978-0-9810344-1-6

Advent and Psychic Birth
by Mariann Burke, Revised Ed., Trade Paperback, 170pp, 2014
— ISBN 978-1-926715-99-5

Sea Glass: A Jungian Analyst's Exploration of Individuation & Suffering
by Gilda Frantz, 1st Ed., Trade Paperback, 240pp, Index, Biblio., 2014
— ISBN 978-1-77169-020-1

Transforming Body and Soul
by Steven Galipeau, Rev. Ed., Trade Paperback, 180pp, Index, Biblio., 2011
— ISBN 978-1-926715-62-9

Lifting the Veil: Revealing the Other Side by Fred Gustafson & Jane
Kamerling, 1st Ed., Trade Paperback, 170pp, Biblio., 2012
— ISBN 978-1-926715-75-9

Resurrecting the Unicorn: Masculinity in the 21st Century
by Bud Harris, Rev. Ed., Trade Paperback, 300pp, Index, Biblio., 2009
— ISBN 978-0-9810344-0-9

The Father Quest: Rediscovering an Elemental Force
by Bud Harris, Reprint, Trade Paperback, 180pp, Index, Biblio., 2009
— ISBN 978-0-9810344-9-2

Like Gold Through Fire: The Transforming Power of Suffering
by Massimilla & Bud Harris, Reprint, Trade Paperback, 150pp, Index,
Biblio., 2009 — ISBN 978-0-9810344-5-4

The Art of Love: The Craft of Relationship by Massimilla and Bud Harris, 1st Ed., Trade Paperback, 150pp, 2010
— ISBN 978-1-926715-02-5

Emily Dickinson: A Medicine Woman for Our Times by Steven Herrmann, 1st Ed., Trade Paperback, 290pp, Index, Biblio., 2018
— ISBN 978-1-77169-041-6

Divine Madness: Archetypes of Romantic Love by John R. Haule, Rev. Ed., Trade Paperback, 282pp, Index, Biblio., 2010
— ISBN 978-1-926715-04-9

Tantra and Erotic Trance in 2 volumes by John R. Haule

Volume 1 - Outer Work, 1st Ed., Trade Paperback, 215pp, Index, Bibliography, 2012 — ISBN 978-0-9776076-8-6

Volume 2 - Inner Work, 1st Ed., Trade Paperback, 215pp, Index, Bibliography, 2012 — ISBN 978-0-9776076-9-3

War of the Ancient Dragon: Transformation of Violence in Sandplay by Laurel A. Howe, 1st Ed., Trade Paperback, 166pp, Index, Biblio., 2016 — ISBN 978-1-77169-034-8

Eros and the Shattering Gaze: Transcending Narcissism by Ken Kimmel, 1st Ed., Trade Paperback, 310pp, Index, Biblio., 2011
— ISBN 978-1-926715-49-0

A Jungian Life by Thomas B Kirsch, 1st Ed., Trade Paperback, 224pp, 2014
— ISBN 978-1-77169-024-9

The Motherline: Every Woman's Journey to Find Her Female Roots by Naomi Ruth Lowinsky, Reprint, Trade Paperback, 252pp, Index, Biblio., 2009 — ISBN 978-0-9810344-6-1

The Sister From Below: When the Muse Gets Her Way by Naomi Ruth Lowinsky, 1st Ed., Trade Paperback, 248pp, Index, Biblio., 2009 — ISBN 978-0-9810344-2-3

The Rabbi, The Goddess, and Jung: Getting the Word from Within by Naomi Ruth Lowinsky, 1st Ed., Trade Paperback, 242pp, Index, Biblio., 2017 — ISBN 978-1-77169-036-2

The Dairy Farmer's Guide to the Universe in 4 volumes by Dennis L. Merritt:

Volume 1 - Jung and Ecopsychology, 1st Ed., Trade Paperback, 242pp, Index, Biblio., 2011 — ISBN 978-1-926715-42-1

Volume 2 - The Cry of Merlin: Jung the Prototypical Ecopsychologist, 1st Ed., Trade Paperback, 204pp, Index, Biblio., 2012
— ISBN 978-1-926715-43-8

Creases in Culture: Essays Toward a Poetics of Depth
by Dennis Patrick Slattery, 1ˢᵗ Ed., Trade Paperback, 424pp, Biblio., 2014
— ISBN 978-1-77169-006-5

Our Daily Breach: Exploring Your Personal Myth Through Herman Melville's Moby-Dick by Dennis Patrick Slattery, 1ˢᵗ Ed., Trade Paperback, 424pp, Biblio., 2015 — ISBN 978-1-77169-029-4

The Guilt Cure
by Nancy Carter Pennington & Lawrence H. Staples, 1ˢᵗ Ed., Trade Paperback, 200pp, Index, Biblio., 2011 — ISBN 978-1-926715-53-7

Guilt with a Twist: The Promethean Way
by Lawrence Staples,1ˢᵗ Ed., Trade Paperback, 256pp, Index, Biblio., 2008
— ISBN 978-0-9776076-4-8

Our Creative Fingerprint
by Nancy Carter Pennington & Lawrence H. Staples, 1ˢᵗ Ed., Trade Paperback, 92pp, Index, Biblio., 2017— ISBN 978-1-77169-040-9

The Creative Soul: Art and the Quest for Wholeness
by Lawrence Staples, 1ˢᵗ Ed., Trade Paperback, 100pp, Index, Biblio., 2009
— ISBN 978-0-9810344-4-7

Deep Blues: Human Soundscapes for the Archetypal Journey
by Mark Winborn, 1ˢᵗ Ed., Trade Paperback, 130pp, Index, Biblio., 2011
— ISBN 978-1-926715-52-0

The Dream: The Vision of the Night
by Max Zeller, Rev. Ed., Trade Paperback, 202pp, 2015
— ISBN 978-1-77169-028-7

Phone Orders Welcomed
Credit Cards Accepted
International call +1-307-222-9575
www.fisherkingpress.com

www.ingramcontent.com/pod-product-compliance
Lightning Source LLC
Chambersburg PA
CBHW040148270326
41929CB00025B/3434